Excel® 2007 Macros

Made EASY

John S. Hambleton
38 Sandwood Drive
Marquette, MI 49855

Excel® 2007 Macros
Made EASY

Gail Perry

Mc
Graw
Hill

New York Chicago San Francisco Lisbon
London Madrid Mexico City Milan New Delhi
San Juan Seoul Singapore Sydney Toronto

The *McGraw·Hill* Companies

Library of Congress Cataloging-in-Publication Data

Perry, Gail.
  Excel 2007 macros made easy / Gail Perry.
    p. cm.
  Includes index.
  ISBN 978-0-07-159958-0 (alk. paper)
  1.   Microsoft Excel (Computer file) 2.   Macro instructions (Electronic computers) 3.   Electronic spreadsheets.
  4.   Microsoft Visual Basic for applications. I. Title.
  HF5548.4.M523P3856 2009
  005.54—dc22

                                                                                    2008041751

McGraw-Hill books are available at special quantity discounts to use as premiums and sales promotions, or for use in corporate training programs. To contact a special sales representative, please visit the Contact Us page at www.mhprofessional.com.

Excel® 2007 Macros Made Easy

1234567890   DOC DOC   0198

ISBN   978-0-07-159958-0
MHID   0-07-159958-4

Sponsoring Editor	**Acquisitions Coordinator**	**Indexer**	**Illustration**
Roger Stewart	Carly Stapleton	Broccoli Information	International Typesetting
Editorial Supervisor	**Technical Editor**	Management	and Composition
Patty Mon	Greg Kettell	**Production Supervisor**	**Art Director, Cover**
Project Manager	**Copy Editor**	Jean Bodeaux	Jeff Weeks
Harleen Chopra,	Margaret Berson	**Composition**	
International Typesetting	**Proofreader**	International Typesetting	
and Composition	Paul Tyler	and Composition	

About the Author

Gail Perry is a CPA, financial journalist, and the author of more than 20 books on financial software, taxes, and personal finance. She is the managing editor for *AccountingWEB*, a contributing editor for *SMB Finance* magazine, and an instructor.

Contents at a Glance

Chapter 1   Recording Macros   1

Chapter 2   Editing Macros   19

Chapter 3   Creating Macros in Visual Basic   35

Chapter 4   Storing Macros   53

Chapter 5   Understanding Macro Commands   73

Chapter 6   Using Visual Basic Subroutines
                   and Creating Functions   91

Chapter 7   Creating Interactive Macros   103

Chapter 8   Using Macros to Format Cells   119

Chapter 9   Using Variables in Macros   133

Chapter 10   Creating If/Then/Else Routines   147

Chapter 11   Exploring Loops   157

Chapter 12   Adding Controls to Your Worksheets   171

Index   183

Introduction

Welcome to *Excel 2007 Macros Made Easy*! This book was written for everyday Excel users, like yourself, who want to free themselves from the drudgery of repeating the same tasks over and over again. In this book, you'll learn powerful shortcuts and time-saving methods for expediting and remembering tasks. Unlike other books in this series, it is focused on teaching you just the things you need to know to get up and running with spreadsheet macros quickly and easily. You won't need to have a degree in programming or to set aside hours and hours for study to be able to get through the lessons in this little book and put them to work for you right away. In fact, you should be able to create your first macro in about a minute.

Inside this book, you'll discover how to teach Excel to do repetitive tasks that take up valuable time and energy that you could spend on more productive endeavors. You'll also learn how to protect the integrity of your data by creating macros that prevent incorrect information from being entered into your spreadsheets. Using Excel macros, you can even interact with other users, asking them to input specific data. So, get ready to jump in! It's time to let Excel macros free you from drudgery and make your work life smoother and easier.

Elements Used in This Book

Reading page after page of unbroken text, especially in a how-to book, can be deadly dull. I tried to guard against that by providing lots of illustrations along the way to help you see what you need to be doing on your computer, as well as to provide visual interest. I also added a number of special elements to this book and others in the *Made Easy* series that set off important additional information and help you quickly find what you need when you refer back to the book. Here's what they are:

- **Briefing**   Short, individually titled sidebars on topics that provide you with important background information related to the tutorial

- **Memo**   Marginal notes, tips, and reminders that drive home a point, provide useful advice, or warn you about potential hazards

- **The Easy Way**   Handy groupings of tips that provide lists of shortcuts or tricks that make accomplishing tasks even easier

- **FAQ**   Brief answers to groups of frequently asked questions about the topic at hand

- **Links**   Pointers to useful external resources for software downloads, news and information, and technical resources

Recording Macros

The easiest way to create a macro in Excel is by recording your steps with Excel's macro recorder. Then, the next time you want to perform these steps, you simply turn on the previously recorded macro and sit back with a nice cup of tea while you watch the macro do your work for you.

For example, if you would like to automate a task in Excel, you record yourself performing the task by turning on a little virtual tape recorder, which will record each step as you enter it. When you are finished entering your steps, you turn off the recorder, and presto! You have a macro! Well, almost. There are a few pieces of technical housework that must be performed, such as naming the macro and deciding where to store it, but for all practical purposes, macro recording is a fairly simple business.

Here are the basic steps for recording a macro:

1. Turn on the macro recorder.

2. Enter a name for the macro.

3. Indicate a desired shortcut key for the macro (optional).

4. Indicate where you want the macro to be stored.

5. Enter a description for the macro (optional).

6. Start the recorder.

7. Enter your steps.

8. Stop the recorder.

Once you have recorded a macro, you can run your macro in one of two ways:

- If you assigned your macro to a key combination, you can press that key combination at any time to run the macro.

- Whether or not you assigned your macro to a key combination, you can access your macro from the ribbon. You'll display a macro list, choose the macro you want to run, and then choose Run.

We'll go through each of these steps of recording and running macros and learn what they mean, while actually recording some real-life macros. Then, later in the chapter, we'll learn how to test your macros, and we'll learn alternative methods for saving and retrieving macros.

Displaying the Developer Ribbon

Macro making is made much easier with the use of the Developer ribbon, a special toolbar designed to help you with creating, running, and revising your macros. You can access some of the macro commands from the View toolbar, but you'll find your macro experiences will be much easier if you have the Developer ribbon on display.

Follow these steps to add the Developer ribbon to your Excel screen:

1. Click the Office button in the top-left corner of your Excel screen. The Office menu appears.

2. Click the Excel Options button at the bottom of the menu window.

3. Make sure the Popular option (see Figure 1-1) is highlighted on the left side of the Excel Options window.

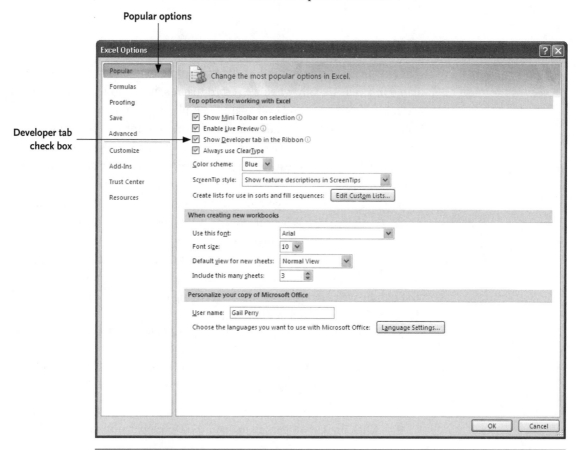

Figure 1-1   Displaying the Developer ribbon

4. Click to check the box Show Developer Tab in the Ribbon.

5. Click OK. The Developer ribbon is now available to you by clicking the Developer tab at the top of your Excel screen.

Note that the Developer ribbon is now a permanent part of your Excel ribbon choices. Should you decide you no longer want to have access to the Developer ribbon, you can go back to the Excel Options window and uncheck the box for the Developer ribbon.

Creating a Macro

The first macro we're going to create is a simple macro that places your name in a cell. Usually when we record macros, we try to record a task that we expect to use over and over again. So if placing your name in a cell is something you'll do a lot, this macro will work well for you by saving you a few keystrokes. If you use a company name frequently on your spreadsheets, or some other familiar text, you can enter that text in this macro instead of your own name.

Here's a phrase you're going to hear over and over again throughout this book: *Take baby steps*. What this means is that, when you're working with macros, every single keystroke, every little step is significant. So when we discuss creating and recording macros, we're not going to skip over any steps. Even if the steps seem obvious (like placing a space between your first and last name), we're going to mention every single step. That way, nothing will be missed, and your macros will be perfect!

So for our first macro, here are the steps to follow—*all* the steps:

1. With your Excel spreadsheet open, place your cellpointer in cell A1. This way, we'll all be in exactly the same place when we start recording this macro.

2. Click the Developer tab to open the Developer ribbon.

3. Click the Record Macro option on the ribbon. Alternatively, you could click the Macro button that appears at the bottom of your Excel screen in the left corner.

4. In the Record Macro dialog box, as shown in Figure 1-2, in the Macro Name field, enter **NAME1** as the name of this macro. There can be no spaces in a macro name.

5. In the Shortcut Key field, hold down the SHIFT key and type **n** so that CTRL+SHIFT+N will be the keyboard shortcut for this macro. (Note: I didn't use CTRL+N for my macro command shortcut because that keyboard shortcut already exists in Excel as the command to open a new workbook. If I pressed CTRL+N for the macro shortcut, I would not receive a warning that CTRL+N already has another use—instead, the macro usage would supersede the original CTRL+N command.)

6. In the Store Macro In field, choose "Personal Macro Workbook." This is the universal workbook that is accessible by all Excel spreadsheets. The other choices are "New Workbook" and "This Workbook." If you choose either of these options, the macro is associated with only one workbook and is not accessible to other workbooks.

7. Enter an optional Description for this macro. You have the option of entering some text describing what the macro does or when it is to be used.

8. Click OK. The macro recorder is now running and will record all of your keystrokes.

9. Back in the spreadsheet, in cell A1, enter your name as you wish to record it in this macro, leaving a space between each word. In my spreadsheet, I have entered "Gail Perry" in cell A1.

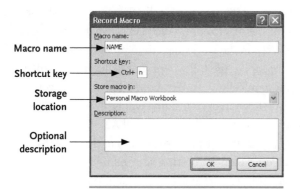

Macro name ➤

Shortcut key ➤

Storage location ➤

Optional description ➤

Figure 1-2   Recording a macro

5

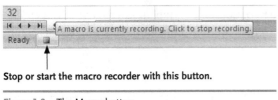

Stop or start the macro recorder with this button.

Figure 1-3   The Macro button

10. Press ENTER when you have finished entering your name. The cellpointer moves to the cell beneath the one where you entered your name (in this case, A2).

11. Click the Stop Recording option on the Developer ribbon. Alternatively, you can click the Macro button at the bottom-left corner of your Excel screen, as shown in Figure 1-3. The macro is now recorded.

Test the Macro NAME1

After recording your macro, you'll want to give it a test drive to make sure that the macro does what you intended.

Follow these steps to test your NAME1 macro:

1. Open a new Excel worksheet and place your cellpointer in cell A1.

2. Press CTRL+SHIFT+N.

3. Your name should now appear in cell A1 and the cellpointer has moved to cell A2. The macro is a success!

What happens if you place your cellpointer in a cell other than cell A1 and press the keyboard shortcut for the macro command? Let's give it a try. Click in any other cell (other than cell A1) on the worksheet, then press CTRL+SHIFT+N. What happens? Your name appears in the cell where your cellpointer resided, but now the cellpointer is sitting in cell A2. In fact, no matter what cell you start in, when you run the NAME1 macro, your name will be entered in the cell where you start, and your cellpointer will return to cell A2.

Why does this happen? If you think back to the creation of the NAME1 macro, you'll remember that you recorded entering your name in cell A1, having already placed your cellpointer in that cell before beginning the recording process. Then you pressed ENTER, and the cellpointer moved to cell A2. The macro recorded just that—the process of entering your name in the currently occupied cell, and then the process of your cellpointer moving to cell A2. So, no matter where you are when you play back this macro, your cellpointer is going to scurry back to cell A2 after entering your name.

A Different Perspective on the Macro

Let's fine-tune the NAME1 macro just a bit. This time, let's say we want to ensure that your name is always entered in cell A1 when you run your macro. We only need to make a small change in the macro in order to accomplish this task. Instead of placing the cellpointer in cell A1 before we begin recording, for our second macro, we're going to turn on the macro recorder *before* moving the cellpointer. In that way, the movement of the cellpointer to cell A1 will become part of the macro.

Here are the steps to follow to create a macro that always places your name in cell A1:

1. Click the Record Macro option on the ribbon.

2. In the Macro Name field, enter **NAME2** as the name of this macro.

3. Let's leave the Shortcut Key field blank for this macro.

4. In the Store Macro In field, choose "Personal Macro Workbook."

5. If you like, enter an optional Description for this macro.

6. Click OK. The macro recorder is now recording your steps.

7. Press CTRL+HOME to send your cellpointer to cell A1.

8. Enter your name as you wish to record it in this macro.

9. Press ENTER when you have finished entering your name. The cellpointer moves to cell A2.

10. Click the Stop Recording option on the Developer ribbon.

Test the Macro NAME2

Open a new worksheet. We'll test this new macro to see if we get the desired results. Click anywhere on the worksheet—try clicking in a cell other than cell A1. Because we didn't assign a keyboard shortcut to this macro, we'll need to access the macro in a different manner.

Follow these steps to run the macro NAME2:

1. Click the Macros button on the Developer ribbon. The Macro window appears.

2. Click the NAME2 macro—it should appear as PERSONAL.XLSB!NAME2.

3. Click the Run button. Your name should now appear in cell A1, and the cellpointer is resting in cell A2.

Yet Another Macro Variation

We've created two name macros and each does something a bit different, but each macro used what we call *absolute references*. Using absolute references, Excel records the exact location where you move your cellpointer. If we use relative references instead, Excel records your cellpointer movement *in relation to* where your cellpointer is on the worksheet. This macro should illustrate the difference between the two types of references. We're going to create one final macro for entering your name. In this macro, we'd like the ability to place your name in *any cell* in the workbook, and have the cellpointer rest in the cell beneath your name when the macro is completed. We'll call this macro NAME3.

Here are the steps for creating the NAME3 macro:

1. Click the Use Relative References option on the Developer ribbon.

2. Click the Record Macro option on the ribbon.

3. In the Record Macro dialog box, in the Macro Name field, enter **NAME3** as the name of this macro.

4. Leave the Shortcut Key field blank for this macro.

5. In the Store Macro In field, choose "Personal Macro Workbook."

6. If you like, enter an optional Description for this macro.

7. Click OK. The macro recorder is now recording your steps.

8. Without moving your cellpointer to a new cell, type your name.

9. Press ENTER when you have finished entering your name. The cellpointer moves to the cell beneath your name.

10. Click the Stop Recording option on the Developer ribbon.

Test the Macro NAME3

Click anywhere on the worksheet—it doesn't matter what cell you click in. Now we'll test NAME3:

1. Click the Macros button on the Developer ribbon. The Macro window appears.

2. Click the NAME3 macro—it should appear as PERSONAL.XLSB!NAME3.

3. Click the Run button. Your name should now appear in the cell where your cellpointer was, and the cellpointer is resting in the cell beneath your name.

4. Experiment by clicking on different cells in the worksheet and running the NAME3 macro. Each time, your name should appear where you want it and the cellpointer rests in the cell below.

Note that when you choose to run a macro, it doesn't matter if the Use Relative References option is turned on or off. This option only affects the macro when it is recording.

Pay attention to the importance of deciding what cells your cellpointer is in both before and after you start recording the macro. Tiny decisions like this form the crux of successful macro writing. You need to develop a mindset where you think of every contingency as you make decisions about how you will create your macros.

As you can see, each of these three macros works differently:

- NAME1 places your name in any cell, wherever your cellpointer is located, and returns the cellpointer to cell A2 when it is finished.

- NAME2 places your name in cell A1, no matter from which cell you run the macro. Your cellpointer returns to cell A2 when the macro is finished.

- NAME3 places your name in any cell, wherever your cellpointer is located, and returns the cellpointer to the cell beneath your name.

These little macros are simple, performing only one task. The differences between these macros are subtle, but significant. As we progress through the rest of this book, learning more about how macros are recorded and created, you'll see that the issues addressed in these three macros will be considered frequently.

Simple Date Macro

Using the knowledge you've gained already in this chapter, let's create a simple macro that puts today's date in the cell of your choice. First, decide how you want the date to appear. There's already a built-in formula in Excel that places today's date in a cell. But that date isn't static—it changes each time you reopen the spreadsheet. Suppose you want *today's* date in a cell, you want the date to remain permanently in the cell without updating, and you want it to appear in a format like this:

February 2, 2008

First, decide how you would enter the date if you were typing it. Remember, *baby steps*. I think I would first click on the cell where I want the date to appear. Then I'd use the TODAY formula to enter today's date. But that formula uses a format of 2/2/08, and I want to see the format I displayed above. So next I'd need to change the format of the cell to the date style I prefer. But I've still got a problem—that cell is going to update every time I open the worksheet. I want the date to remain static. So next I'm going to copy the date to the clipboard. Finally, I'll use the Paste Special command to paste the value of the cell into the cell itself, replacing the formula. Finally, I'll press ESC to empty the clipboard. This actually takes quite a few steps. That's why I want a macro to do this for me, so I don't have to go through all of those steps in the future when I want to assign a static date to a cell. Here goes:

1. Click in the cell where you want the date to appear.

2. Click the Developer ribbon.

3. Click to turn off the Use Relative References feature if it is activated—we don't need that feature for this macro.

4. Click the Record Macro button.

5. In the Record Macro dialog box (see Figure 1-4), enter a macro name (I've used TodaysDate—remember, you can't use spaces).

6. Store this macro in the Personal Macro Workbook.

7. Enter an optional description.

8. Click OK.

9. Now it's time for the steps described in the beginning of this section. First, click the Formulas ribbon.

10. Click the Date & Time option.

11. Click TODAY.

12. In the Function Arguments box that appears, click OK.

13. Right-click on the date.

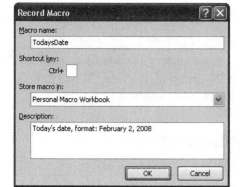

Figure 1-4   Recording the date macro

14. Choose Format Cells from the pop-up menu.

15. Click the Date category in the Format Cells window.

16. Choose March 14, 2001 as the Type. (Note: There is a list of Date types available on the Home ribbon, but this particular type does not appear on that list.)

17. Click OK. Your date now appears correctly. But this date still incorporates the TODAY function, which means that it will change if you open the worksheet tomorrow. So, we're not done yet.

18. Click the Home ribbon.

19. Click the Copy option. (Note: You could also have right-clicked on the date and chosen Copy from the pop-up menu.)

20. On the Home ribbon, click the arrow under the Paste option.

21. Choose Paste Values. Notice that the value in the Formula bar changes from TODAY() to today's actual date.

22. Press ESC.

23. Click the Developer ribbon.

24. Click Stop Recording.

Whew! Twenty-four steps to put a date in a cell. Aren't you glad we've recorded this task for future use? Try out your macro by clicking in another cell, clicking the Macros option on the Developer ribbon, and clicking the TodaysDate macro, then clicking the Run button. Nice date.

Formatting with Macros

Here's another easy but repetitive task that you can automate with a macro. Say you have a little worksheet that you prepare each month. The titles and formatting and formulas on the worksheet are unchanging, month after month. Often what you do when it's time for a new worksheet is to open last month's worksheet, delete the numbers, save it as this month's worksheet, and fill in this month's numbers. I wouldn't be surprised if at least once you deleted last month's numbers and saved the new numbers for this month using the name for last month's worksheet. Oops!

By creating the skeleton for your worksheet as a macro, with formulas and formatting and titles, it's an easy task to open a new worksheet file, play back your macro to set up the sheet, and then drop in this month's numbers safely, without having to worry about saving over last month's information.

Let's try it. Figure 1-5 shows the very simple worksheet we'll create.

Here is a summary of the steps required to create this worksheet: On an empty worksheet, enter Month: in cell A1, then enter the city names Chicago, Peoria, and Danville in cells B2, C2, and D2. Enter Total in cell E2. Make these totals bold as you enter them. Enter the titles Sales, Expenses, and Profit in cells A3, A4, and A5. Make these titles bold as you enter them. In cell B5, enter a formula to subtract sales from expenses. Copy the formula to C5 and D5. Enter a SUM formula to add cells B3 through D3 and enter the result in cell E3. Copy the formula to cells E4 and E5.

Here are the steps for recording this as a macro called MonthlyReport. Notice that I avoided using my mouse to drag over cells for formatting or creating formulas.

	A	B	C	D	E	F
1	Month					
2		Chicago	Peoria	Danville	Total	
3	Sales				0	
4	Expenses				0	
5	Profit	0	0	0	0	
6						

Figure 1-5 Simple worksheet

MEMO

You might think that a template is a good alternative tool for creating a worksheet skeleton, and you'd be right. However, the advantage of using a macro for this task is that you can call up the worksheet skeleton anywhere using the macro, even in an existing worksheet.

1. With a blank worksheet open, click the Developer ribbon.

2. Turn on the Use Relative References feature.

3. Click Record Macros.

4. Enter **MonthlyReport** as the name of this macro.

5. Save the macro in the Personal Macro Workbook.

6. Enter a description if you want to.

13

7. Click OK.

8. Enter **Month:** in cell A1.

9. Enter **Chicago** in cell B2. Return to B2 and press CTRL+B to make the title bold.

10. Enter **Peoria** in cell C2 and make it bold; enter **Danville** in cell D2 and make it bold; enter **Total** in cell E2 and make it bold.

11. Enter **Sales** in cell A3 and make it bold; enter **Expenses** in cell A4 and make it bold; and enter **Profit** in cell A5 and make it bold.

12. Arrow over to cell B5.

13. Type an equal sign (=) and then arrow to B3, type a hyphen (-), and then arrow to B4. Press ENTER to complete the formula.

14. Copy the contents of cell B5 (I used CTRL+INSERT—you can also right-click and choose Copy, or click Copy on the Home ribbon).

15. Paste to cells C5 and D5.

16. Arrow over to cell E3.

17. Enter the formula **=SUM(**, and then arrow over to B3, hold down your SHIFT key, and arrow over to cell D3.

18. Press ENTER.

19. Copy the contents of cell E3 down to cells E4 and E5.

20. Click the Developer ribbon and turn off the macro recorder, or click the Macro button in your taskbar to turn off the recorder.

Test your macro first by entering data in the worksheet to make sure the formulas work, and then by clicking elsewhere on your worksheet or on a new worksheet and running the MonthlyReport macro to display your report skeleton.

MEMO

If any of your macros don't work, don't worry about that at this point. We will discuss debugging macros in the next chapter.

14

Saving Macros

When you created your three NAME macros, you were given three options for saving the macros. We chose to save all three of the macros to the Personal Macro Workbook. This workbook loads automatically when you open Excel, and it is available to all workbooks, so these three macros are now available to all of your Excel workbooks, including workbooks you might have created and saved previously.

Saving to the Personal Macro Workbook

You'll find that when you attempt to close Excel, you will receive a message asking if you want to save the changes you made to your Personal Macro Workbook. If you click Yes, your macros will be saved and available to you the next time you open Excel.

The Personal Macro Workbook is a hidden workbook, not normally accessible as a workbook you can view. The file name is Personal.xlsb. Later in this book we'll talk more about the Personal Macro Workbook.

Saving to This (the Current) Workbook

Another option is to save the macros to *this workbook*. Some macros relate to specific workbooks and aren't of use in other workbooks. For example, if you create a macro that offers the user the option of performing certain calculations on the data in an existing workbook, and the calculations relate only to that workbook, there is no need to make the macro universally available in the Personal Macro Workbook. Instead, you would save a macro like this to the current workbook.

When you choose to save a macro to your current workbook, you must also save the workbook in order to keep the macro. When you are ready to save a workbook that contains a macro, you must choose Macro-Enabled Workbook as your workbook type. When the Save As window appears, follow these steps:

1. Choose the folder where you want to save the workbook in the Save In field (see Figure 1-6).

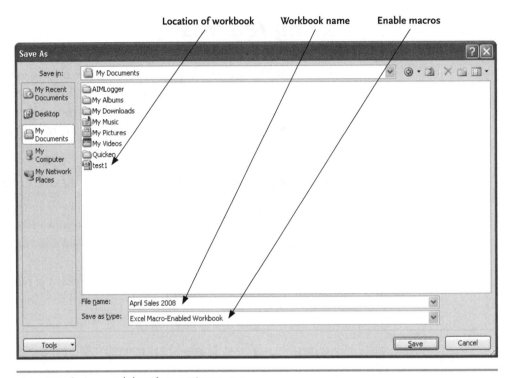

Location of workbook   **Workbook name**   **Enable macros**

Figure 1-6   Saving a worksheet that contains macros

2. Enter the workbook name in the File Name field.

3. Choose Excel Macro-Enabled Workbook in the Save as Type field.

4. Click Save.

Saving to a New Workbook

The third option is to save a macro to a *new workbook*. Some people want to create macros that are available to them for use in other workbooks, but they don't want to make them available universally through the Personal Macro Workbook. By saving macros in a new workbook, you choose when you want the macro to be available by simply opening that workbook.

MEMO

Caution! It will appear that there is nothing in this new workbook! However, when you try to save the new workbook, you will be prompted to save the workbook as a macro-enabled workbook.

MEMO

Note that if you choose not to save the new workbook, your new macro will be lost.

As soon as you choose to save your macro to a new workbook, Excel opens a new workbook on your screen. Excel gives the new workbook the name *Book* followed by a number. If you previously have only opened one workbook in this Excel session, the new workbook is called Book2, until you save it and give it a new name. If you previously have opened two workbooks, the new workbook is called Book3, and so on.

When you want to use the macro that has been saved to a new workbook, you must open that workbook. As long as that file is open, your macro will be available to all Excel workbooks that are open on your computer.

In Chapter 2, "Editing Macros," we take a look at the inner workings of macros and learn how to edit and correct problems in macros we've already created.

17

Editing Macros

In this chapter we're going to talk about making simple corrections and changes to macros that you have recorded. We'll use the Visual Basic Editor to access the macros you have already created in Chapter 1. We'll look at those macros, study the way in which they were created, and do some easy editing. Later in the book we'll learn about designing macros from scratch by using the Visual Basic Editor, and that will be important because many macros can't be recorded and instead have to be written out, step by step. By the time we're ready to work on writing macros, you'll be comfortable with the Editor, and the idea of designing a macro by typing the commands won't seem daunting.

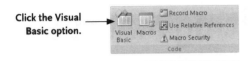

Click the Visual Basic option.

Figure 2-1   The Code group on the Developer ribbon

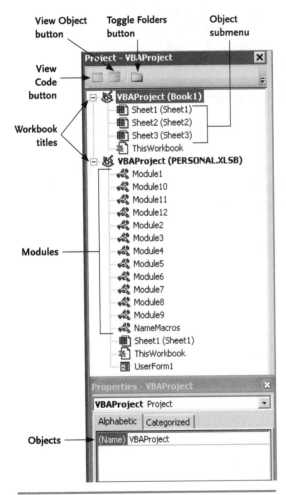

Figure 2-2   The Project Explorer

Open the Visual Basic Editor

Opening the Visual Basic Editor is so easy that you can do it in one step:

1. In the Code group on the Developer ribbon, as shown in Figure 2-1, click Visual Basic.

That's it—you've opened the Editor!

Examine the Visual Basic Editor

Let's take a little tour of the VB Editor because this screen looks quite a bit different from your normal Excel worksheet. We'll look at some of the elements of the Editor with which you'll want to be familiar.

Project Explorer

The Project Explorer appears on the left side of the Visual Basic screen, as shown in Figure 2-2. If you don't see the Project Explorer, choose View | Project Explorer from the menu, or press CTRL+R. The Explorer displays a list of all workbooks currently open in Excel, including the Personal Macro Workbook (PERSONAL.XLSB), which is always open but is a hidden workbook. The Microsoft Excel objects appear as a submenu. Beneath each Workbook title are entries for each sheet in the workbook and one entry for the entire workbook. Clicking on any of the sheet

> Double-clicking on a module name opens a code window that displays the code for all macros that reside within that module.

names or on the This Workbook entry allows you to see a list of the *properties* associated with that sheet or workbook in the Properties window (which will be explained in more detail in the section "Properties Window" later in this chapter). If macros have been created within the workbook (and we created several macros in Chapter 1 that are housed in the Personal Macro Workbook), you will see a submenu for modules beneath the workbook title (Module1, Module2, and so on). The modules contain procedures (macros) that Excel can execute.

There are three buttons at the top of the Project Explorer. Click the View code button to display a code window on the right side of your VB screen. (The Code window will be explained in more detail in the section "Code Window" later in this chapter.) If the code window is already displayed, clicking this button does nothing. Note that you must select a module first in order to activate this button. Click the View Object button with an object selected (such as one of the sheets or workbooks displayed in the project list), and the code for that object appears. For example, you can quickly display Sheet1 of Book1 by clicking on that sheet name and then clicking the View Object button. The Toggle Folders button alternately hides and shows the folders in the Project window.

Modules

The modules are where the macros are stored. If you've created macros that were saved to a particular workbook, that workbook will have a module associated with it and that module will appear in the Project Explorer when that workbook is open. The Personal Macro Workbook contains modules as well, and the code for the macros you created in Chapter 1 resides in these modules. You can click once on a module name and click the View Code button to display the code.

Properties Window

The Properties window displays the attributes that are associated with the various Excel workbooks and sheets that are displayed in the Project Explorer.

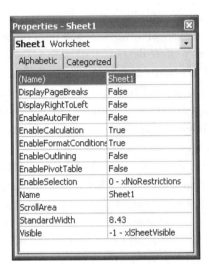

Figure 2-3   Attributes of the selected workbook

If the Properties window isn't visible on your screen, choose View | Properties Window from the VB menu, or just press F4. There are two tabs in the Properties window, Alphabetic and Categorized, as shown in Figure 2-3. Each tab lists the same information, just in a different order. Click on a worksheet or workbook in the Project Explorer and you will see the properties associated with that worksheet or workbook in the Properties window. A module doesn't have any properties associated with it (other than its name).

Code Window

The code window displays the Visual Basic code associated with the item that is selected in the Project Explorer. You can double-click on an item in the Project Explorer to view the code associated with that item. For example, in Figure 2-4, the code for the macros stored in Module 3 of the Personal Macro Worksheet is displayed.

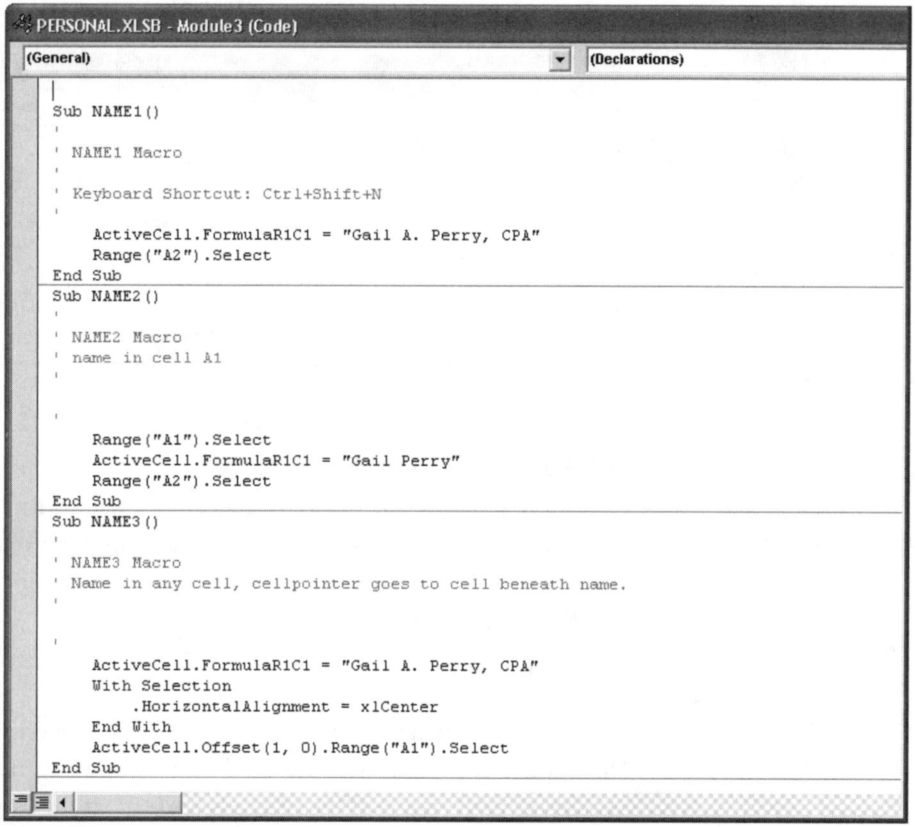

```
PERSONAL.XLSB - Module3 (Code)

(General)                                              (Declarations)

Sub NAME1()
'
' NAME1 Macro
'
' Keyboard Shortcut: Ctrl+Shift+N
'
    ActiveCell.FormulaR1C1 = "Gail A. Perry, CPA"
    Range("A2").Select
End Sub
Sub NAME2()
'
' NAME2 Macro
' name in cell A1


'
    Range("A1").Select
    ActiveCell.FormulaR1C1 = "Gail Perry"
    Range("A2").Select
End Sub
Sub NAME3()
'
' NAME3 Macro
' Name in any cell, cellpointer goes to cell beneath name.


'
    ActiveCell.FormulaR1C1 = "Gail A. Perry, CPA"
    With Selection
        .HorizontalAlignment = xlCenter
    End With
    ActiveCell.Offset(1, 0).Range("A1").Select
End Sub
```

Figure 2-4   Macro code in the code window

Learning to Read Macros

Let's examine the three NAME macros that we created in Chapter 1. These macros are quite similar to one another, but each one provides us with an opportunity to learn some of the basics of how the macro programming language works. Figure 2-5 shows the code for the NAME1 macro.

Start of Sub procedure

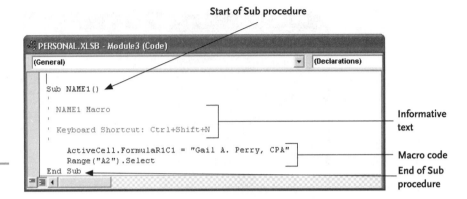

Informative text

Macro code

End of Sub procedure

Figure 2-5   The NAME1 macro

NAME1 Macro

As you recall, the NAME1 macro created in Chapter 1 involved you placing your cellpointer in cell A1 before recording, and then you turned on the recorder, entered your name, and pressed ENTER. Looking at the macro code for NAME1, this is what we see:

```
* Sub NAME1()
```

Each macro that performs a task is called a *Sub procedure*. The first line of a Sub procedure begins with the word Sub followed by the name of the macro. In this case, the name of the macro is NAME1. If the macro were called "ProductMenu," the first line would read:

```
Sub ProductMenu()
```

After the macro name is a pair of parentheses. If the macro requires some particular information in order to perform its task, that information, called *arguments*, is listed inside the parentheses.

As you look at the macro in the code window, you'll notice that some lines begin with apostrophes and other lines don't begin with an apostrophe.

MEMO

In addition to macros, you can record user-defined functions in the Visual Basic Editor. Functions begin with the word Function instead of Sub. Functions are discussed in Chapter 3.

Comment Lines

Several lines that follow the Sub Name line begin with an apostrophe. This apostrophe distinguishes the lines as informative text that does not affect the operation of the macro, often called *comments*. Information you might see in this comment area includes the name of the macro, any optional description information you entered when you created the macro, and a keyboard shortcut associated with the macro. In the case of the NAME1 macro, the descriptive information includes a line showing the name of the macro and a line showing the keyboard shortcut of CTRL+SHIFT+N. You are allowed to write additional information here. As long as you begin your lines with an apostrophe, you can enter comments that will not impact the operation of the macro.

Command Lines

The lines that follow the informative information in Figure 2-5 are the command lines. This is the part of the macro that contains the Visual Basic code language that runs the operation of the macro. Depending on the complexity of the macro and the number of commands the macro must perform, this area might be quite short (NAME1 has only two lines of code) or quite lengthy. Let's look more closely at the command lines included in the NAME1 macro.

```
ActiveCell.FormulaR1C1 = "Gail A. Perry, CPA"
```

ActiveCell refers to the cell in which your cursor resides. FormulaR1C1 means that for purposes of this macro, the active cell is designated as Row 1 Column 1 (R1C1). This is the point from which this macro is launched, so any references to cell movement in the macro would be made in relation to this cell, the cell in the first row, and the first column from which your cellpointer is starting. No matter what cell you designate as the active cell when you begin running this macro, that cell is considered to be R1C1 for purposes of this macro. See the discussion about the macro, NAME3, in the section "NAME3 Macro," for more information on this statement. In the NAME1 macro, this information is not used.

```
= "Gail A. Perry, CPA"
```

The information in quotation marks, `"Gail A. Perry, CPA"`, is the information that this macro will place in the cell.

```
Range("A2").Select
```

`Range` refers to the range of cells that will be selected in this macro.

`("A2")` is the specific range of cells to which this command line is referring. So the range of cells "A2" refers to the single cell, A2.

`Select` is what the macro has been instructed to do with the specified range of cells. In this case, the macro instruction is to select cell A2.

`End Sub` is always the last line of a macro.

In addition to learning the basic macro commands we've seen in our NAME1 macro, you should also examine the format of the macro. The first and last lines appear at the left margin. The apostrophes that appear to the left of the informational text also appear at the left margin. The macro command lines are indented.

You will be able to see the nuances that accompany the slight change in commands for macros NAME2 and NAME3.

NAME2 Macro

The difference between the NAME1 and the NAME2 macros is that when we recorded the NAME1 macro, we began by placing our cellpointer in cell A1 before recording. The NAME2 macro in the VB Editor (see Figure 2-6) is nearly the same as the NAME1 macro, except for these differences:

- There is no keyboard shortcut for NAME2.

- There is a bit of descriptive text for NAME2 ("name in cell A1").

- There is one additional command in NAME2:

  ```
  Range("A1").Select
  ```

This code that appears as the first line of code in NAME2 is the code that was recorded when we moved the cellpointer to cell A1 after turning on the macro recorder.

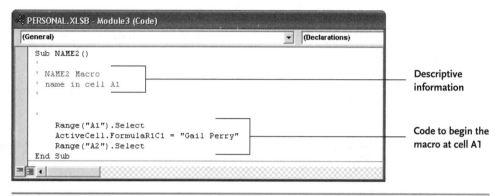

Figure 2-6   The NAME2 macro

NAME3 Macro

The difference between the NAME3 macro and the other macros is that the NAME3 macro works from any location, instead of either assuming the user will put the cellpointer in cell A1 or forcing the cellpointer to go to cell A1. With NAME3, the user begins with the cellpointer in any cell, runs the macro, and the cellpointer ends at the cell beneath the starting cell. The code that places the name in the cell (`ActiveCell.FormulaR1C1 = "Gail Perry"`) remains the same throughout all three macros. Notice the slight difference in the code for the NAME3 macro shown in Figure 2-7.

The last line contains this code:

```
ActiveCell.Offset (1, 0).Range ("A1").Select
```

This `Offset` command indicates cursor movement. The macro command is indicating that the new active cell is the cell one row down and 0 columns to the right (1, 0) of the previous cell. The statement `Range ("A1").Select` indicates that, for purposes of this macro, the new cellpointer location will be referred to as cell "A1." This cell location can be anywhere on the worksheet, depending on where your cellpointer is when you run the NAME3 macro, but as far as the macro is concerned, your new cell location is cell A1, and this is how the cell will be referred to if there is any additional macro code added to this macro.

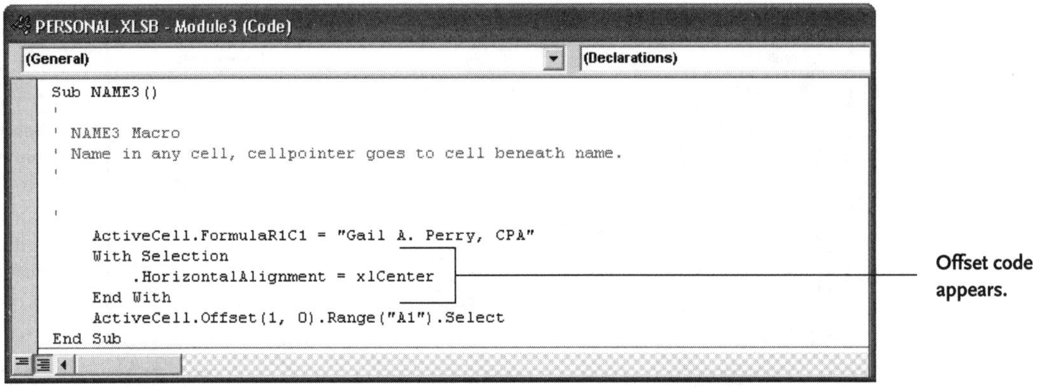

```
PERSONAL.XLSB - Module3 (Code)

(General)                                          ▼   (Declarations)

    Sub NAME3()
    '
    ' NAME3 Macro
    ' Name in any cell, cellpointer goes to cell beneath name.
    '


    '
        ActiveCell.FormulaR1C1 = "Gail A. Perry, CPA"
        With Selection
            .HorizontalAlignment = xlCenter
        End With
        ActiveCell.Offset(1, 0).Range("A1").Select
    End Sub
```

Offset code appears.

Figure 2-7   The NAME3 macro

Editing Macros

It's easy to make editing changes in the macros you see in the VB Editor. You can type in the macros just as you would in any document, keeping in mind of course that, when typing actual command code, you must use actual Visual Basic commands. But you can change the name of a macro, you can enter or change explanatory information in the comment areas of the macro, and you can change, add, and remove macro code.

Here's an easy change. Let's say you want to change the name you used in the NAME3 macro. I entered my name, "Gail Perry," but maybe instead I want to use my middle initial and my professional designation: "Gail A. Perry, CPA." (Or perhaps you misspelled your name and you want to correct the spelling!) I can edit the name as it appears on the first line of macro code to read the way I want it to:

```
ActiveCell.FormulaR1C1 = "Gail A. Perry, CPA"
```

If I go to a worksheet page and run the macro, NAME3, the change will have already taken place and the revised name appears on my worksheet.

28

Saving an Edited Macro

Even though you make a change in your macro and you test the macro and see that the change has been recorded, there is one more step necessary to saving a macro. That change you made will be effective in any of your worksheets, as long as you don't close Excel. As soon as you try to close Excel, you will be asked if you want to save the changes you made to the Personal Macro Workbook. You must answer **Yes** to this question if you want your changes to be permanently saved.

Click here to save.

Figure 2-8 Save changes made in Visual Basic.

Instead of waiting to save your macros when you exit Excel, you can save at any time right in the Visual Basic screen by using either of these techniques:

29

- Press CTRL+S.

- Click the Save icon on the Visual Basic toolbar (see Figure 2-8).

Finding Help in Visual Basic

When you have questions, you'll find that there is ample help available to you in the Visual Basic Editor.

- If you want additional information about any of the code that appears in your macro, right-click on a code line and choose Quick Info. Each item of code is considered to be an *object*. When you ask for Quick Info, a balloon appears with information about what type of object this is.

- You can find more detailed information about the Visual Basic objects in the Object Browser. From within the Visual Basic Editor, press F2, choose View | Object Browser from the menu, or click the Object Browser button on the toolbar (see Figure 2-9).

Object Browser button

Figure 2-9   The Visual Basic toolbar

Enter command or   Click to perform   Click on
statement here.   search.   results.   Help

The Object Browser window appears, as shown in Figure 2-10. Enter the command or statement you want to explore in the Search Text field. Click the binoculars button to perform the search. When the results appear, click the statement or command in the results list, and then click the Help button for more information.

■ Another way to get into the Visual Basic Help system is to choose Help | Microsoft Visual Basic Help from the menu. Enter the name of the object about which you want additional information, and then click Search. Alternatively, you can enter the information for which you are searching in the Help field on the far right side of the VB toolbar, where it says "Type a question for help" (see Figure 2-11), and then press ENTER.

Enter your question here.

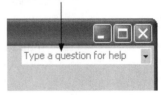

Figure 2-10   The Object Browser window leads to more help.

Figure 2-11   Quick access to Excel Help

30

When you examine the Help information for a VB object, you'll see a definition, some narrative text of how the object can be used, an example of VB code using the object, and a description of the results that will be produced.

- You can search the contents of the Excel Developer Reference material, and you might find this better organized and less overwhelming than searching all through the Help system. Choose Help | Microsoft Visual Basic Help from the menu, or press F1. The Excel 2007 Developer Reference appears. Click Excel Object Model Reference. Here you'll see a detailed list of VB objects. Click an object and drill down to find additional information about that object.

- One of the best ways to learn about the usage of VB objects is to record macros as we did in Chapter 1 and then study the resulting code in the VB Editor. By examining the code associated with a macro that successfully performs the steps you recorded, you approach your learning session already knowing what the code does. Then it's simply a matter of familiarizing yourself with which code statements perform which tasks.

Easiest Way to Get Help

Let's say we want to go back to the NAME3 macro and, in addition to entering our name in a cell, we want the macro to center the name in the cell. We need to determine the macro command for centering text. You can find what you're looking for in the Excel Developer Reference, but first it helps to know that cell alignment, such as left, center, and right, is considered to be *horizontal alignment*. Knowing this, you can work your way through the Developer Reference to finally find the screen that describes how to assign the value of center to the horizontal alignment. But there is a much easier way: Record a macro!

At any time, you can record a macro that performs a task. Then examine the macro in the VB Editor, find the code you need, and copy and paste that code into your existing macro. After that, you can delete the sample macro you created because you no longer need that.

THE EASY WAY

Your VB window is most likely still open. Pressing ALT+TAB will allow you to quickly flip over to the VB window.

For the example of centering text, follow these steps:

1. Head back to your worksheet (click the View Microsoft Excel button at the far left side of the VB toolbar).

2. Turn on the macro recorder (Developer ribbon, Record Macros).

3. Name this macro Test1, and save it in *this* workbook. There's no need to use the Personal Macro Workbook for this macro—we won't need access to this macro from any other worksheet.

4. With your cellpointer in any cell, display the Home ribbon, and then click the Center Text button. There doesn't have to be any text in the cell in order to perform this task, and it doesn't matter which cell you use. All we're doing here is harvesting code.

5. Display the Developer ribbon and click Stop Recording.

6. Click the Visual Basic button to return to the VB Editor.

7. You'll see that a module for the current workbook has been added in the Project window. Double-click that module to display the code window. The Test1 macro appears (see Figure 2-12).

8. Notice that there are several attributes that have been assigned to the selection in the Test1 macro. Whenever you apply a formatting change such as the centering command to a cell, the associated macro code shows a group of attributes. For our situation, we only need the code for centering text. That would be

```
With Selection
    .HorizontalAlignment = xlCenter
End With
```

The rest of the formatting statements are not a necessary part of the command to center text in a cell.

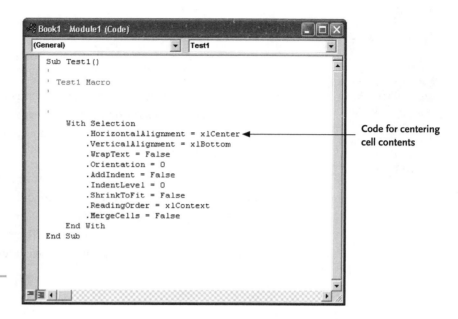

Figure 2-12 Macro code for cell formatting

9. Copy and paste the three lines of code shown in step 8 above into your NAME3 macro, beneath the line that describes the content of the ActiveCell and before the line that contains the Offset command. (I copied and pasted the entire block of code, and then deleted the lines I didn't need.) Your NAME3 macro will now look like this (with your name in place of mine):

```
Sub NAME3()
'
' NAME3 Macro
' Name in any cell, cellpointer goes to cell beneath name.
'
'
    ActiveCell.FormulaR1C1 = "Gail A. Perry, CPA"
    With Selection
```

```
            .HorizontalAlignment = xlCenter
    End With
    ActiveCell.Offset(1, 0).Range("A1").Select
End Sub
```

10. Go back to your worksheet and test the Name3 macro by clicking in any cell, clicking Macros on the Developer ribbon, choosing NAME3, and clicking Run. You'll see that your name appears in the current cell, and it is centered.

11. You no longer need the Test1 macro. Return to the VB Editor and in the Project window, right-click on the module containing that macro, and choose Remove Module1. You'll be asked if you want to export the module before removing it. Answer **No**. The module is gone, the Test1 macro is gone, and you've cleaned up the clutter.

Creating Macros in Visual Basic

We're going to enter the world of macro building the easy way—using the principles we've already begun exploring in Chapters 1 and 2. In this chapter we'll create several useful macros as we continue to familiarize ourselves with Visual Basic. Since the point of this book is to learn macro construction at a comfortable and understandable pace, this chapter will focus on recording macros and then using the recorded code to make new macros.

Since you already know how to perform many tasks in Excel (I'm taking it for granted that if you're ready to build macros, you've already mastered the basics), we'll take advantage of the knowledge you already possess to create macros that can make your Excel experiences easier, more efficient, and more rewarding.

First, we'll create macros that perform some repetitive tasks. There are two types of repetitive tasks:

- The tasks you perform frequently, in different worksheets

- The tasks that require repetition within a single worksheet

We're primarily concerned with the first type of repetitive task here. When we get to Chapters 10 and 11, we'll learn about macros that repeat themselves within a single worksheet.

In addition, we'll learn about applying what we know about macros to create customized functions.

Display Formulas as Values

There are times when you want to make a worksheet available to someone else who doesn't need to see the formulas that are used to calculate the numbers on the sheet. This macro enables you to quickly remove formulas from selected cells. After you've applied the macro, the value that appears in the Formula bar is the same as the value in the cell; no formula appears in the worksheet.

Begin by opening a worksheet that contains formulas. The worksheet in Figure 3-1 has formulas that calculate the commission for various salespeople and those formulas are confidential, so we want to hide the calculation in the Bonus column.

The first step in creating a macro should be to think through the process of how the procedure should be accomplished. Remember to use baby steps! To change the formula in a cell to a value, here are the steps I would follow:

1. Click on the cell containing the formula.

2. Copy the formula to the clipboard (click the Copy button on the Home ribbon).

3. Open the Paste menu (click the Paste arrow on the Home ribbon).

Paste arrow

Change this formula to a value.

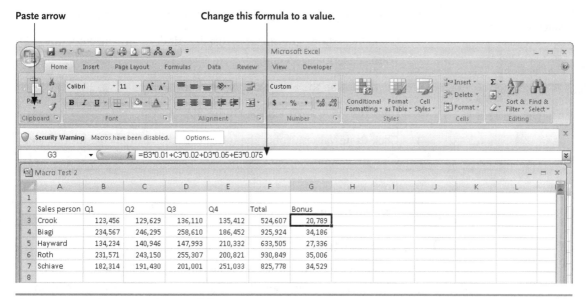

G3 =B3*0.01+C3*0.02+D3*0.05+E3*0.075

	A	B	C	D	E	F	G
1							
2	Sales person	Q1	Q2	Q3	Q4	Total	Bonus
3	Crook	123,456	129,629	136,110	135,412	524,607	20,789
4	Biagi	234,567	246,295	258,610	186,452	925,924	34,186
5	Hayward	134,234	140,946	147,993	210,332	633,505	27,336
6	Roth	231,571	243,150	255,307	200,821	930,849	35,006
7	Schiave	182,314	191,430	201,001	251,033	825,778	34,529
8							

Figure 3-1   Formulas appear in the Formula bar.

4.   Choose Paste Values.

5.   Remove the marquee indicating the cell contents are still in the clipboard (press ENTER or ESC).

Now that I've figured out the steps, it's time to record that process in a macro. Here are the steps to automate this process and make the macro available to other worksheets:

MEMO

We're selecting the cell before recording the macro—we don't want the macro to make a cell selection for us.

1.   With the worksheet containing formulas open, click on a cell that contains a formula that you want to hide.

2.   Click Record Macro on the Developer ribbon. There's no need to use relative references for this macro because we want to be able to apply the macro on a cell-by-cell basis, not have it relate to specific cells.

3.   Name the macro. I've used FormulaToValue.

MEMO

Changing a cell from formula to value is a permanent process. Once the formula is removed, there's no going back to display the formula again.

4. Make sure the macro is going to the Personal Macro Workbook.

5. Click OK. I didn't give this macro a description—the macro name seems descriptive enough.

6. Click Copy on the Home ribbon.

7. Click the Paste arrow on the Home ribbon.

8. Click Paste Values. Notice the formula in the Formula bar immediately changes to a value.

9. Press ESC.

10. Turn off the macro recorder.

Test the Macro

Give your macro a trial run: Click on a cell containing a formula, click the Macros button on the Developer ribbon, choose FormulaToValue, and then click Run.

Now let's try selecting a range of cells and running the macro again. Just as you can select a range of cells and perform other operations, you can use your macro in the same way. Highlight a range of cells containing formulas, and then click Macros, and choose FormulaToValue. All of your highlighted cells now contain just the values and the formula no longer appears.

View the Macro Code

It's time to take a look at this macro in the Visual Basic Editor. Click the Visual Basic button on your Developer ribbon. The code for your macro will be located in one of the modules of the Personal Macro Workbook. You'll see the Personal Macro Workbook in the Project window. You can view the code in the modules within that workbook by double-clicking on the module names in the Project window. Alternatively, you can choose Tools | Macros in the VB Editor, set the Macros In field to VBAProject (PERSONAL.XLSB), and when you see the macro you want to view in the Macro Name list, click on it, and then click the Edit button.

Here's the code that appears:

```
Sub FormulaToValue()
    Selection.Copy
    Selection.PasteSpecial Paste:=xlPasteValues,
Operation:=xlNone, SkipBlanks _
        :=False, Transpose:=False
    Application.CutCopyMode = False
End Sub
```

Examining the code, we see that the first line of code under the macro name, `Selection.Copy`, copies the selected cell to the clipboard. Next the Paste Special command is executed, but look at all of the statements that follow `Selection.PasteSpecial`:

```
Paste:=xlPasteValues,
Operation:=xlNone,
SkipBlanks:=False,
Transpose:=False
```

All of these statements represent the baggage that comes along with using the Paste Special command in Visual Basic. The only command that actually executes a change in the worksheet is the `Paste:=xlPasteValues` command. The rest of the commands are superfluous and are unnecessary in the execution of this macro. You can remove the rest of the commands if you want to clean up your macro code, but it does no harm to leave them there.

The last line of the code, `Application.CutCopyMode = False`, is the command that was recorded when you pressed the ESC key. This command removes the information from the clipboard and removes the marquee from the selected cell(s).

If you want to experiment further, you can remove the excess baggage (the `Operation`, `SkipBlanks`, and `Transpose` lines) information from the macro and then test the macro again. You'll see that the macro works fine and removes the formulas from your cells, replacing them with values. The cleaned-up macro code will look like this:

```
Sub FormulaToValue()
' FormulaToValue Macro
    Selection.Copy
    Selection.PasteSpecial Paste:=xlPasteValues
    Application.CutCopyMode = False
End Sub
```

Make One Macro out of Little Macros

Looking at the new ribbons in Excel, you can see that Microsoft has made many commands available to you with the quick click of a mouse. Commands that you once had to search through menus to find are now visible on the ribbons. But even though the commands are visible, you still have to execute some steps to use them. First, you have to figure out which ribbon your command is on, and then you have to search for the command icon or look through the little drop-down menus that appear here and there on the ribbons. Some commands can be found on the context menu (the pop-up shortcut menu) or the mini-toolbar that appears when you right-click in the worksheet.

If you routinely use several commands when creating or editing worksheets, save yourself time by placing those commands in a macro. That way, each time you open a new worksheet, if you need to apply these changes, you can do so all at once by running one macro. You can try recording a macro using all of the commands at once, but you might find it's easier to record each command separately and then put all the commands together into one macro in the VB Editor.

For this exercise, we'll record macros that execute these tasks:

- Set the gridlines so they will print
- Change page orientation from portrait to landscape
- Expand the column width to 10

Record the Little Macros

The first macro we're going to record will turn on the gridlines for purposes of printing the workbook. Typically, the gridlines are for display only—they don't print unless you ask for them. Turning on the printable gridlines requires you to check the Print Gridlines feature on the Page Layout ribbon.

1. Turn on the macro recorder.

2. Let's call this macro Gridlines.

3. Save the macro in *this workbook*. We're not going to need this little macro—we'll harvest the code we need and then we can delete the macro when we close the workbook without saving.

4. Click OK.

5. Click the Page Layout ribbon.

6. In the Sheet Options area of the ribbon, check the Print box beneath the Gridlines feature (see Figure 3-2).

7. Turn off the recorder.

41

Figure 3-2 Changing sheet options

Click to check the Print Gridlines box.

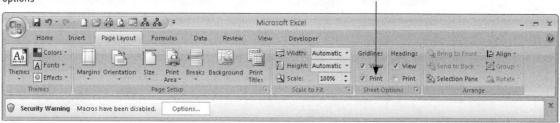

MEMO

You might be wondering what you should do if, when you displayed the Page Layout ribbon, the Print Gridlines box was already checked. The macro recorder is running but you can't perform the task. Go ahead and click in the Print Gridlines box. This will have the effect of *unchecking* the Print box. No matter. We'll fix this up in the VB Editor.

Next we'll record a macro to change the page orientation from Portrait (default) to Landscape. To perform the task in Excel, we activate the Page Layout ribbon, click the arrow for Orientation choice, and then click Landscape, as shown in Figure 3-3. So let's record this:

1. Turn on the macro recorder.

2. Name: **Landscape**. Location: This workbook.

3. Click the Page Layout tab.

4. Click the Orientation arrow.

5. Click Landscape.

6. Turn off the recorder.

As you can see, this process of recording macros is really quite easy. We've got one more macro to record, and then it's time to put our project together into one macro we can use repeatedly. For this final macro, we want to expand our column width so that it will display 10 characters (as opposed to the default 8.43 characters). We need to decide how many columns will get this designation. The easiest way to proceed is to change the width of the columns on the entire worksheet. That way we're covered for any number of columns that might be needed. Therefore, when recording this macro, we'll select the entire worksheet, and then make the column adjustment so that all columns are affected. Finally, we'll add a step to click on cell A1 so that the selection of the entire workbook will be turned off. Here are the steps:

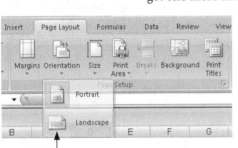

Click the Landscape option.

Figure 3-3   Changing orientation

1. Turn on the macro recorder.

2. Name: **ColumnWidth**. Location: This workbook.

3. Click the Select All box that appears above the row number 1 and to the left of Column A.

4. Right-click over a column letter and choose Column Width from the shortcut menu.

5. In the Column Width dialog box (see Figure 3-4), enter **10** for the new width.

6. Click OK.

7. Click on cell A1.

8. Turn off the macro recorder.

Test the Macros

Before proceeding, let's test our macros to make sure they do what they're supposed to do. Open a new workbook. On the Developer ribbon, click Macros, select the Gridlines macro, and then click Run. Repeat these steps with the Landscape and the ColumnWidth macros. If there is a problem running any of the macros, you'll be redirected to the VB Editor with an error message. Rather than trying to debug these little macros, the easiest thing to do is delete the macro code in the VB Editor, return to your worksheet, and re-record the macro.

Select All box.

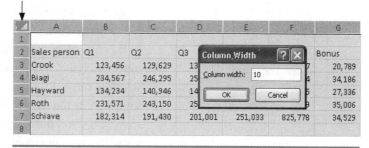

Figure 3-4   Setting a new column width

MEMO

Do not close
your workbook!
Your macros are
stored there!

Harvesting Macro Code

Now that we're ready to start assembling a macro that will accomplish all that
we did in the three little macros, we'll need to leave the friendly confines of
the workbook screen and open the VB Editor. On the Developer ribbon, click
the Visual Basic button, or press ALT+F11, and the VB Editor appears.

As you recall, we stored the little macros in the current workbook. We
haven't even given that workbook a name, and that's all right because, when
we're finished, there will be no need to save it or the macros associated with it.
You'll see your workbook, and any other workbooks you might have open, listed
in the Project Explorer window of your VBA screen as shown in Figure 3-5.
If the Project Explorer window doesn't appear, choose View | Project Explorer
in the VB Editor, or press CTRL+R.

We need to find the little macros that you created. See the workbook
you were using? It's a VBAProject, listed in the Project Explorer window. If
you named the workbook, that name appears in
parentheses. If the workbook is unnamed, you'll
see (Book1) or (Book2) or whatever workbook
number you were using. The macros are stored in
the module accompanying the workbook. You'll
see the module listed in the menu beneath the
workbook title.

Double-click on the module to open the
module's code window. Scroll through the
window and you will see that your little macros
are all there. Those macros don't look so little,
do they? We're going to see that there is a lot of
code material in those macros that we don't need.
To create our new macro, we're going to copy, or
harvest, only the code that we need.

As you scroll through the macros, you'll see
that each one begins and ends with a Sub line. You'll also note that there is a

**Macros are stored
in the modules.**

Figure 3-5 The Project
Explorer

horizontal line separating each macro—that makes it easy to see where one macro ends and the next begins.

Open a New Module

We need to find a place to put our new macro. Depending on how many macro sessions you've had already and how much of your previous work you've saved, there might be several modules or just a couple of modules in the VBAProject (PERSONAL.XLXB) area of the Project Explorer. Most or all of those modules probably already have some code stored in them. You can add to one of those modules, but just to keep things neat and clean, let's open a fresh new module.

Click on the title of the Personal Macro Workbook (VBAProject (PERSONAL.XLXB)), and then choose Insert | Module from the menu. A new module is listed under the Personal Macro Workbook, and a new, empty code window appears.

Arrange Your Module Windows

The new window probably appears right on top of the other module code window, the one that contains your code for the little macros. Slide the title bars of the module's windows around and resize the windows so that you can see both the new Personal Macro Workbook module window and the workbook module that contains your code from the little macros (see Figure 3-6).

Construct Your New Macro

We're ready to start making a macro in the VB Editor, using the pieces of code we will harvest from the three little macros that we recorded. Here are the steps to constructing your new macro:

1. Enter the word **Sub** followed by a name for your new macro, followed by a set of opening and closing parentheses. I've decided to name my new macro MyWorksheetSetup. Remember, there can be no spaces in your macro name.

45

```
Macro Test 2.xlsm - Module2 (Code)

(General)                              Gridlines

Sub Gridlines()
'
' Gridlines Macro
'


'
    With ActiveSheet.PageSetup
        .PrintTitleRows = ""
        .PrintTitleColumns = ""
    End With
    ActiveSheet.PageSetup.PrintArea = ""
    With ActiveSheet.PageSetup
        .LeftHeader = ""
        .CenterHeader = ""
        .RightHeader = ""
        .LeftFooter = ""
        .CenterFooter = ""
        .RightFooter = ""
```

```
PERSONAL.XLSB - Module11 (Code)

(General)                              (Declarations)
```

Figure 3-6   The Code windows

THE EASY WAY

You can copy and paste the title line from an existing macro into the new module window, and then overwrite the name of the copied macro with your new macro name.

2. Press ENTER when the first line of your macro is in place. Surprise! The last line of your macro—End Sub—appears automatically. All of the code you enter will be placed between these two lines of text.

3. Enter some comment lines beneath the title line of the macro. Begin a comment line with an apostrophe. This way the macro program won't mistake your comments for macro code and try to interpret commands from your comments. On the comment lines you can describe your macro. As you press ENTER after each line of comment, you'll see that the comment line changes color to distinguish it from the programming code.

MEMO

You can enter as many comment lines as you like in a macro—just be sure to begin each one with an apostrophe. You can enter blank lines if you want to add some space between the comments and the code.

MEMO

The With...End With construction is a common feature of VBA macros. Whenever you see a statement beginning with With, remember that the whole statement ends with the End With line, and so the entire collection of information between these two lines is part of the same command.

4. We're ready to place some code in this macro. Let's start with the code from the Gridlines macro. Notice there are three sections in the code of the Gridlines macro. The first section begins with With ActiveSheet.PageSetup and ends with End With.

   ■ The first With...End With command contains code regarding printing title rows and columns. This has nothing to do with printing gridlines, and so we can ignore this code segment of the Gridlines macro.

   ■ The next line, ActiveSheet.PageSetup.PrintArea = "", is a command regarding the print area of the worksheet. Notice there is no command between the quotation marks. This line of code doesn't perform any operation and is unnecessary to the process of printing the gridlines.

   ■ The third section of the code in the Gridlines macro contains another With...End With statement. This one contains many lines of command. Search down to the line that says .PrintGridlines = True. This is the command that we're looking for, and the command needs to be flanked by the With...End With statements. The rest of the code just explains the default page setup features and, since none of these features will change (other than the Gridlines command), this code is not necessary to the operation of this macro. Here's the code that is significant for us:

```
With ActiveSheet.PageSetup
    .PrintGridlines = True
End With
```

5. You can copy those particular lines of code and paste them into the new macro. Or, you can copy and paste the entire block starting with the second With ActiveSheet.PageSetup line of code and ending with the End With code, and then delete all the lines of code that are not required for this macro.

47

MEMO

You also have the option of simply typing the lines of code into the new macro, but I don't recommend this. As easy as typing might sound, it's even easier to mistype some of the text or miss a punctuation mark. Don't take chances with your code. By copying and pasting, you'll ensure that your code is exactly correct.

6. Figure 3-7 shows the macro so far.

7. At this point there is enough code entered in the new macro for you to perform a test. You have the correct macro structure in place, with the Sub and End Sub lines, and there is a complete macro command in the macro. You can wait until we're finished to test the macro, or you can to go a new worksheet and take a test drive now. If you decide to test the new macro, open a new worksheet, click Macros on the Developer ribbon, choose MyWorksheetSetup, and click Run. Then click the tab for the Page Layout ribbon and you will see that the Print Gridlines box has been checked.

8. We're ready for the next piece of code in our new macro, so return to the VB Editor if you're not there already. Find the Landscape macro. This time we're looking for the code that changes the orientation from portrait (default) to landscape. Again, we've got the two With... End With sections of the macro and a stand-alone command line regarding the print area. In the second With...End With section, find the code for orientation:

```
.Orientation = xlLandscape
```

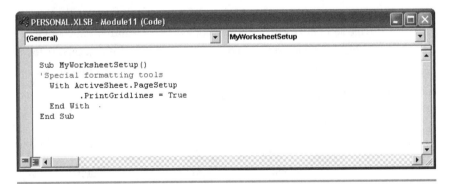

Figure 3-7   The macro code after adding the first little macro

Notice that the With...End With statements that flank this code are identical to the statements that appeared in the Gridlines macro. Guess what this means? You don't have to repeat these statements in your new macro. You can repeat these command lines if you want to, and add the following code to your new macro:

```
With ActiveSheet.PageSetup
    .Orientation = xlLandscape
End With
```

Or, you can save yourself some code lines and place the orientation code within the existing With...End With statement, like this:

```
With ActiveSheet.PageSetup
    .PrintGridlines = True
    .Orientation = xlLandscape
End With
```

9. We've got one more piece to add to our macro—the command to widen margins to 10 characters. Find the ColumnWidth macro and look at the code that appears there:

```
Cells.Select
Selection.ColumnWidth = 10
Range("A1").Select
```

The first line of code is the command to select all the cells in the worksheet. The second line orders Excel to take the selection (all the cells) and change the column width to 10. The final line of code moves the cellpointer to cell A1 and selects that cell. Remember, we did this so that the entire worksheet won't remain selected when the macro stops running.

These three lines of commands need to be added to your new macro. They will follow the End With statement that already appears in your macro. Remember you can copy and paste these command lines. The final macro looks like this:

```
Sub MyWorksheetSetup()
'
' Macro contains basic setup commands including
```

```
' turning off the gridlines, changing to landscape
' and increasing column width to 10 characters.
'
    With ActiveSheet.PageSetup
        .PrintGridlines = True
        .Orientation = xlLandscape
    End With
    Cells.Select
    Selection.ColumnWidth = 10
    Range("A1").Select
End Sub
```

It's rather amazing to look back at all of those lines of code in the little macros we recorded and see that we only need such a small collection of code lines to accomplish our tasks.

Test Your New Macro

It's time to put the proverbial pedal to the metal and see how our new macro runs. Head back to your workbook area (ALT+F11 gets you there quickly), and open a new workbook. Click the Developer tab, click Macros, and find your new macro on the list. Click the MyWorkbookSetup macro, and then click Run.

All of the changes are now effective in your new workbook. Double-check by opening the Page Layout ribbon and looking at the orientation and the Print Gridlines command. Then right-click on any column letter and select Column Width. You'll see that the column width is now set to 10. All of your changes should be in place. If the macro didn't work as planned, go back to the VB Editor, and examine the precise information that is in the macro. It should match the example given in the preceding section. Make any necessary changes.

Remove Old Macros

You don't need to keep those little macros that you created in the process of making the new macro. In fact, it's wise to remove the macros if there's a chance you changed some elements (for example, cutting and pasting text

Click to delete the
selected macro.

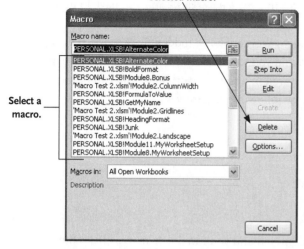

Select a
macro.

instead of copying and pasting—which would have been fine for creating your new macro, but which would prevent the little macro from doing its job). The purpose of creating the little macros was simply to provide elements of code for our new macro. They have served their purpose and are no longer needed.

In the VB Editor, you can very simply remove the old macro code by highlighting the code and deleting it.

Here's another way to delete a macro. Return to the workbook that contains the macros. On the Developer tab, click the Macros button. In the Macro Name box (see Figure 3-8), click the name of a macro you no longer want, and then click the

Figure 3-8 Weeding out unwanted macros

Delete button. You'll be asked if you want to delete the macro. Click Yes (see Figure 3-9) and the macro is removed.

Finally, you can delete unwanted macros by simply removing the workbook that contains the macros. If you close the workbook without saving, everything associated with that workbook is deleted, including its macros.

Figure 3-9 Click Yes to delete a macro.

Deleting Macros from the Personal Macro Workbook

As long as we're on the subject of deleting macros, this is a good time to mention that the process of deleting macros from the Personal Macro Workbook is a bit trickier.

You can open the list of macros, as we did in the last example, and click on a macro that is located in the Personal Macro Workbook, and then click

Delete, but that won't get you too far. A message appears telling you that you are attempting to edit a macro in a *hidden workbook* and you have to *unhide* the workbook.

Because the Personal Macro Workbook is a hidden workbook, an extra layer of protection is added and your macros are just a little bit safer than they would be if they were stored in a regular workbook. You can unhide the Personal Macro Workbook by following these steps:

1. Display the View ribbon.

2. Click the Unhide button.

3. Choose PERSONAL.

4. Click OK.

Now the workbook is unhidden and you can delete macros from the Macros option on the Developer ribbon.

When you are finished deleting macros, be sure to re-hide the Personal Macro Workbook. With the Personal Macro Workbook as your active window, click the Hide button on the View ribbon and the worksheet will go back into hiding.

Another, perhaps easier, method of deleting macros in the Personal Macro Workbook is to go into the VB Editor and delete code. You don't have to unhide/hide the worksheet to make changes in the VB Editor.

When you attempt to close Excel, you will be asked if you want to save the changes that have been made to the Personal Macro Workbook. By all means, answer Yes! Not only will any deletion changes be saved, but all of the macros you created during this session will be saved. Otherwise, if you close Excel and decide not to save the changes that have been made to the Personal Macro Workbook, it's time to go back to the beginning of this chapter and start over!

Storing Macros

Before we go much further with macro development, we ought to get a handle on how to save and keep track of our macros. Before you know it, you'll have dozens of macros and you're going to want to have some easy ways to find and use the macros you've created.

If you've been following along in this book since the beginning, you have created a handful of macros that are stored in the Personal Macro Workbook. In addition, you created some macros that belonged to a particular workbook, and then those macros disappeared when we decided not to save that workbook. You've got a few different choices when deciding where to save your macros:

- Save macros to the Personal Macro Workbook. These macros are available universally to all of your workbooks.

- Save macros to the active workbook that you're using when you create the macro. These macros will always be available to any other workbooks as long as the workbook file containing the macros is open, and of course these macros will always be available to anyone using the workbook in which they are contained.

- Save macros to a workbook dedicated to particular macros. Creating macro workbooks enables you to organize your macros in whatever way makes sense for you and your Excel experiences. You can open a macro workbook whenever you want to use the particular macros stored therein.

Deciding Where to Store Macros

Now that you know you have choices regarding where macros are to be stored, you can start thinking about how you want to organize your macros. Do you want to keep macros in categories, such as macros used to format worksheets, macros that help you organize data, macros for work, macros for hobbies, and so on? Or do you want to have certain macros available to you for all of your Excel projects? Do you have macros that you only use when you're working in one particular worksheet? Answering these questions will help you decide where you want to save your macros.

The decision of where to save a macro is made when you begin creating the macro. If you're recording a macro, you choose a location in the Record

Macro dialog box. If you're creating a macro in the VB Editor, you open a module in the workbook where you want the macro to be stored and enter the code in the code window associated with that module.

Save Macros in the Personal Macro Workbook

Most of the macros we've created so far reside in the Personal Macro Workbook. These macros are available to you whenever you open Excel and in every worksheet you're using. You don't have to search for them and you don't have to open any particular files in order to find them.

When you make any changes to the Personal Macro Workbook, whether you record a new macro, edit an existing macro, create a new macro in the VB Editor, or remove a macro entirely, you will need to save your changes. You can save your changes from within the VB Editor. Make sure your mouse pointer is located somewhere within the Personal Macro Workbook, either on a code window, on one of the elements of the Personal Macro Workbook in the Project window, or in the Properties window with an element of the Personal Macro Workbook displayed. Then choose File | Save Personal.XLSB from the menu (see Figure 4-1). All changes you have made during this session will be saved. If you're planning on spending a lengthy amount of time performing tasks in the VB Editor, it makes sense to save your workbook in this way frequently (not just the Personal Macro Workbook, but any workbook where you are making changes).

Alternatively, you can close the VB Editor without saving and nothing will be lost. Later, when you attempt to close your Excel program, you will see a message asking if you want to save the changes you made to the Personal Macro Workbook. Clicking Yes saves all of your work.

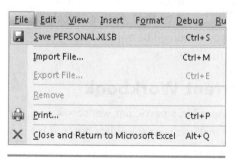

Figure 4-1   Saving the Personal Macro Workbook

Use Workbooks for Macros

Macros that relate to particular types of Excel usage might be best stored in workbooks dedicated to that usage. Whenever you need to do formatting, for example, you can open the workbook containing the formatting macros. Then you go about your formatting on other worksheets, and you'll have access to all the macros you need.

An advantage to storing macros in separate workbooks is that they're portable. You can copy a file containing your macros and give that file to someone else, and your macros will be available on that other person's computer. Another advantage to storing macros in individual workbooks is that you can organize your macros by topic and avoid putting so many macros in the Personal Macro Workbook that it's difficult to sort through them all.

Under the new file-naming rules for Excel 2007, workbooks must be saved as *macro-enabled* files in order to take advantage of the macros saved within them. Macro-enabled files are named with an XLSM extension instead of the normal XLSX extension that applies to typical Excel workbooks. Try to save a workbook containing macros without specifying that you want the XLSM file extension, and you'll receive a message (see Figure 4-2) explaining that by saving the workbook without making it macro-enabled, you will save the workbook as a macro-free workbook. All macros associated with that workbook will be lost.

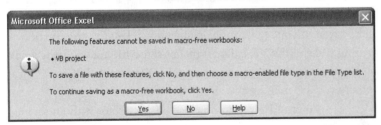

Figure 4-2   Clicking Yes saves the file without macros.

When saving a macro-enabled workbook, choose File | Save and the Save As dialog box appears. Enter the file name that you want to use, and then click the down arrow in the Save as Type field. Choose Excel Macro-Enabled Workbook, the file extension you need will be applied, and your macros will be saved and available for future use.

Save Macros in the Current Workbook

Macros that are of limited use can be stored in a particular workbook. For example, if you create a worksheet that analyzes sales data entered by salespeople and produces reports using that data, you might write a macro that allows you to ask the salespeople to enter the data that is required for those reports and then generate the reports. That macro would be of little use outside that particular worksheet, so it makes sense to store that macro within the workbook.

Another example is the one we saw in Chapter 3. We created macros exclusively for the purpose of harvesting coded material and had no need to keep the macros beyond that limited use, so storing them in the current worksheet made sense, and then the macros that were no longer needed were deleted when the worksheet was closed without saving.

Using Modules in VBA

Quite simply, a *module* is the place where macro code resides. You can think of the modules as extra worksheets; however, they aren't visible unless you're in the Visual Basic Editor, where you can view the contents of all modules associated with any open workbooks as well as the modules associated with the Personal Macro Workbook.

The names of the modules can be changed in the Visual Basic Editor, so, once you start making macros of your own, you can organize the macros by placing them on particular module sheets and naming the sheets with meaningful names.

Rename a module by clicking once on the module to select it, double-clicking the module name in the Properties window, and then entering a new name. For example, I renamed the module containing all of the Name macros that were created in Chapter 1, NameMacros (see Figure 4-3).

Here are some of the things you can do with modules:

MEMO

If the Properties window does not appear in the VB Editor, choose View | Properties Window from the menu, click the Properties Window button on the toolbar, or press F4.

- View the contents of any module by double-clicking on the module in the Project window.

- Insert a new module by choosing Insert | Module from the menu.

- Copy a module from one workbook to another by dragging the module to another workbook in the Project window. The copied module will have the same name as the original.

57

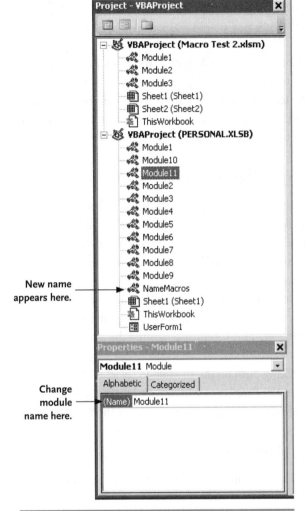

New name appears here.

Change module name here.

Figure 4-3   Renaming modules

Making Macros Available to Others

Previously we discussed the option of saving macros within a workbook. When macros reside within a workbook, you can give the workbook to someone else, and that person will then have access to the macros. Note that the user will have to agree to enable the macros in order to use the macros in the workbook.

In order to copy macros to another workbook, you need to have both the receiving workbook and the workbook that contains the macros open on your computer. (If the macros are in your Personal Macro Workbook, that workbook is already open.) Follow these steps to copy a macro to a new workbook.

Click the Macro Security option on the Developer ribbon. The Trust Center window appears (see Figure 4-4). Note which macro setting is currently in place. Choose the option, Enable All Macros (Not Recommended; Potentially Dangerous Code Can Run), and then click OK.

1. Click the Visual Basic button or press ALT+F11 to display the VB Editor.

2. In the Project Explorer window, find the module(s) containing the macro(s) you want to copy.

3. Drag the module(s) to the receiving workbook.

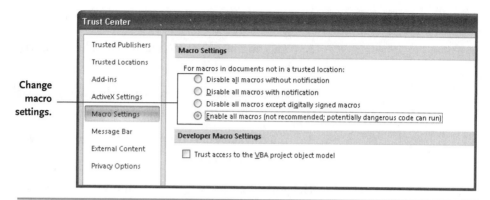

Change macro settings.

Figure 4-4   Enabling macros

4. Press ALT+F11 to return to the worksheets.

5. Open the Trust Center again (see step 1) and return to the macro setting that was in place previously, then click OK.

6. Save the workbook into which you copied the macros with an XLSM file extension.

Protecting Your Macros

There are several reasons why you might want to safeguard your macros. Here are the reasons I came up with—you probably have some more:

■ You worked hard to create your macro—you don't want anyone else changing it or, worse, futzing with the code so that it doesn't work any more.

■ The information in your macros is private—you don't want other users learning the secrets behind how your macros operate.

You have three choices for how you protect your macros:

1. You can make the VBA macros completely inaccessible to everyone but yourself.

2. You can make the macros visible but not changeable to anyone who knows the password that protects them.

3. You can allow only people who know your password the right to change your VBA code.

The protection choice is made within VB Editor. Here are the steps to follow:

1. Click on the project name in the Project window.

2. Right-click and choose VBAProject Properties (this command is also available on the Tools menu).

3. Click the Protection tab in the Project Properties window that appears, as shown in Figure 4-5.

4. Check Lock Project for Viewing if you want to apply a complete lockdown of your VBA macros. No one will be able to edit or even see your macros unless they possess the correct password. Enter the password in the fields provided, then click OK.

5. Alternatively, leave the check box unchecked, but enter a password in the fields provided, if you want to make your VBA macros available for someone who knows the password to view only.

6. Click OK to save your entries.

Check here to restrict viewing and editing VBA code.

60

Enter the password twice.

Figure 4-5   Protecting macros

MEMO

Watch out! Many keyboard shortcuts already exist in Excel. If you choose to utilize an existing keyboard shortcut as your macro shortcut (such as CTRL+B, which is used to turn on the Bold feature), Excel will take you at your word and change the default shortcut to your macro. The shortcut will no longer work for the default command. See the list in the next Briefing for existing Excel keyboard shortcuts.

Assigning Shortcut Keys to Macros

Macros that you only use occasionally probably don't need any special shortcut features. It's easy enough to click the Macros button on the Developer toolbar, view the available macros, click on the one you want, and then click the Run button to execute the macro. That's only three clicks, or four if you have to click the Developer tab—do you need to save more time than that?

Well, apparently the answer is yes, so Excel has an option whereby you can assign your macros to keyboard shortcuts. Once you've assigned the shortcut key combination, you can press the combination on your keyboard and the macro runs, bypassing the Macros menu altogether. That's pretty slick, especially if you prefer using the keyboard to mousing around, but of course the trick is that you have to *remember* the shortcut that you assigned to the macro!

There are three ways to assign a shortcut key to a macro:

- **Recording macros**   Enter the key combination in the Record Macro box. As Figure 4-6 shows, there is a field for Shortcut Key, and the field's label indicates that whatever you enter, your shortcut will include the CTRL key. You can enter a letter or a number in the Shortcut Key box.

61

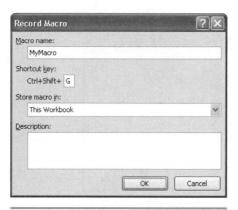

Figure 4-6   Assign keyboard shortcuts when you name your macro.

MEMO

In the VB Editor we have seen that if you assigned a keyboard shortcut when you recorded a macro, that keyboard shortcut appears in the comment section at the top of the macro, right beneath the macro name. You cannot edit the keyboard shortcut information that appears in the VB Editor and expect the keyboard shortcut to change. This information appears as a comment, not a command, so any changes you make to the comment will not alter the shortcut command.

MEMO

Remember! Keyboard shortcuts always start with CTRL and contain only one character—a lowercase letter or a number. You have the option of including the SHIFT key after the CTRL if you want to use a capital letter or a character.

You also have the option of pressing the SHIFT key while entering your letter or number, and then the macro shortcut will be CTRL+SHIFT+whatever key you enter. You can only use one number or letter for your macro shortcuts (or one character, if you're using the SHIFT with the number keys).

■ **Editing macros** Change the keyboard shortcut associated with a macro by first clicking the Macros button on the Developer ribbon. Find the macro whose shortcut you want to change and click once on that macro. Click the Options button. The Macro Options dialog box (see Figure 4-7) appears, displaying the name of the macro, the shortcut key (if any) associated with that macro, and the Description field. In this dialog box, you can change a shortcut key, remove an existing shortcut key, or add a key where none previously existed. Click OK to save your entries.

■ **Creating new VBA macros** When you create a new VBA macro using the VB Editor, there is not an opportunity to assign a keyboard shortcut to the macro. Instead, return to step 2 above—use the Macro Options feature to assign a shortcut to a new macro.

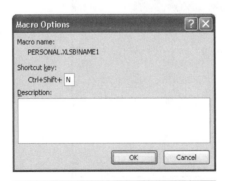

Figure 4-7   Enter, edit, or delete keyboard shortcut.

EXISTING EXCEL KEYBOARD SHORTCUTS

CTRL+SHIFT+(	Unhides any hidden rows within the selection.
CTRL+SHIFT+)	Unhides any hidden columns within the selection.
CTRL+SHIFT+&	Applies the outline border to the selected cells.
CTRL+SHIFT_	Removes the outline border from the selected cells.
CTRL+SHIFT+~	Applies the General number format.
CTRL+SHIFT+$	Applies the Currency format with two decimal places (negative numbers in parentheses).
CTRL+SHIFT+%	Applies the Percentage format with no decimal places.
CTRL+SHIFT+^	Applies the Exponential number format with two decimal places.
CTRL+SHIFT+#	Applies the Date format with the day, month, and year.
CTRL+SHIFT+@	Applies the Time format with the hour and minute, and AM or PM.
CTRL+SHIFT+!	Applies the Number format with two decimal places, thousands separator, and minus sign (–) for negative values.
CTRL+SHIFT+*	Selects the current region around the active cell (the data area enclosed by blank rows and blank columns). In a PivotTable, it selects the entire PivotTable report.
CTRL+SHIFT+:	Enters the current time.
CTRL+SHIFT+"	Copies the value from the cell above the active cell into the cell or the Formula bar.
CTRL+SHIFT+PLUS (+)	Displays the Insert dialog box to insert blank cells.
CTRL+MINUS (–)	Displays the Delete dialog box to delete the selected cells.
CTRL+;	Enters the current date.
CTRL+`	Alternates between displaying cell values and displaying formulas in the worksheet.
CTRL+'	Copies a formula from the cell above the active cell into the cell or the Formula bar.
CTRL+1	Displays the Format Cells dialog box.
CTRL+2	Applies or removes bold formatting.

63

EXISTING EXCEL KEYBOARD SHORTCUTS (CONT.)

CTRL+3	Applies or removes italic formatting.
CTRL+4	Applies or removes underlining.
CTRL+5	Applies or removes strikethrough.
CTRL+6	Alternates between hiding objects, displaying objects, and displaying placeholders for objects.
CTRL+8	Displays or hides the outline symbols.
CTRL+9	Hides the selected rows.
CTRL+0	Hides the selected columns.
CTRL+A	Selects the entire worksheet. If the worksheet contains data, CTRL+A selects the current region. Pressing CTRL+A a second time selects the current region and its summary rows. Pressing CTRL+A a third time selects the entire worksheet. When the insertion point is to the right of a function name in a formula, displays the Function Arguments dialog box. CTRL+SHIFT+A inserts the argument names and parentheses when the insertion point is to the right of a function name in a formula.
CTRL+B	Applies or removes bold formatting.
CTRL+C	Copies the selected cells. CTRL+C followed by another CTRL+C displays the clipboard.
CTRL+D	Uses the Fill Down command to copy the contents and format of the topmost cell of a selected range into the cells below.
CTRL+F	Displays the Find and Replace dialog box, with the Find tab selected. SHIFT+F5 also displays this tab, while SHIFT+F4 repeats the last Find action. CTRL+SHIFT+F opens the Format Cells dialog box with the Font tab selected.
CTRL+G	Displays the Go To dialog box. F5 also displays this dialog box.
CTRL+H	Displays the Find and Replace dialog box, with the Replace tab selected.

EXISTING EXCEL KEYBOARD SHORTCUTS (CONT.)

CTRL+I	Applies or removes italic formatting.
CTRL+K	Displays the Insert Hyperlink dialog box for new hyperlinks or the Edit Hyperlink dialog box for selected existing hyperlinks.
CTRL+N	Creates a new, blank workbook.
CTRL+O	Displays the Open dialog box to open or find a file. CTRL+SHIFT+O selects all cells that contain comments.
CTRL+P	Displays the Print dialog box. CTRL+SHIFT+P opens the Format Cells dialog box with the Font tab selected.
CTRL+R	Uses the Fill Right command to copy the contents and format of the leftmost cell of a selected range into the cells to the right.
CTRL+S	Saves the active file with its current file name, location, and file format.
CTRL+T	Displays the Create Table dialog box.
CTRL+U	Applies or removes underlining. CTRL+SHIFT+U switches between expanding and collapsing of the Formula bar.
CTRL+V	Inserts the contents of the clipboard at the insertion point and replaces any selection. Available only after you have cut or copied an object, text, or cell contents.
CTRL+W	Closes the selected workbook window.
CTRL+X	Cuts the selected cells.
CTRL+Y	Repeats the last command or action, if possible.
CTRL+Z	Uses the Undo command to reverse the last command or to delete the last entry that you typed. CTRL+SHIFT+Z uses the Undo or Redo command to reverse or restore the last automatic correction when AutoCorrect Smart Tags are displayed.

Assigning Macros to the Toolbar

As you know, the old concept of customizable toolbars from earlier versions of Excel no longer exists in Excel 2007. The toolbars with their changeable buttons and the menus with their changeable commands are a thing of the past. Well, almost. There is one area of the Excel command central where you still have some flexibility, and that is the little Quick Access toolbar at the very top of the Excel screen (see Figure 4-8). You don't have total flexibility with this toolbar, but you do have more freedom than you do with the ribbons.

Click here to display menu.

Figure 4-8   Excel's Quick Access toolbar

Add Common Commands to the Toolbar

Customize the Quick Access toolbar by clicking the arrow on the right side of the toolbar. You will see a short menu of some of the most familiar Excel commands, including New, Open, Save, Quick Print, and so on, as shown in Figure 4-9. Commands with a checkmark already appear on your toolbar, Click on any of the unchecked commands to add them to the toolbar.

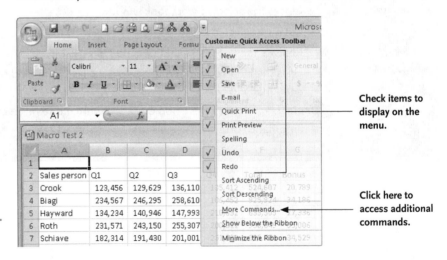

Check items to display on the menu.

Click here to access additional commands.

Figure 4-9   Customizing the Quick Access toolbar

Add Additional Commands to the Toolbar

Customize further by choosing the More Commands option that appears on the Customize menu. In the Excel Options window that appears (see Figure 4-10),

Click here to display the toolbar commands.

Choosing View Macros places the Macros button on your toolbar.

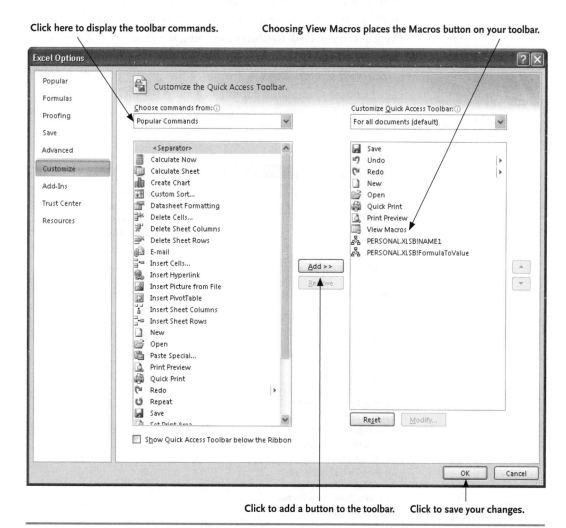

Click to add a button to the toolbar.   Click to save your changes.

Figure 4-10   Choosing buttons to add to the toolbar

click on any command listed on the left side of the window, and then click Add to add the command to the toolbar. One of the commands in the command list is View Macros. Adding this command to the Quick Access toolbar gives you the ability to display the Macros window at any time. Once you've added this command to the toolbar, you save yourself the trouble (if you can call one click trouble) of opening the Developer ribbon before you can display the Macros window.

But wait! There's more! At the top of the list, there is a drop-down menu called Choose Commands From (see Figure 4-10). Click the arrow to display this menu of commands (see Figure 4-11) and you'll see that not only do you

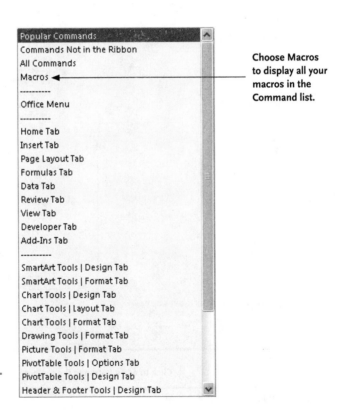

Choose Macros to display all your macros in the Command list.

Figure 4-11   Displaying your macros

have access to *all* Excel commands, any of which can be added to your Quick Access toolbar, but you can click the Macros option and all the macros that reside in your Personal Macro Workbook are displayed in the command list. Choose any macro by clicking on it, then click Add, and you have added the macro to the list of button commands you want to display on your toolbar.

Add Macros to the Toolbar

But wait! There's still more! (I sound like an infomercial, don't I? I'm about to throw in a set of Ginzu knives at no extra charge!). If you add more than one macro to your Quick Access toolbar, you'll see quickly enough that all macros look alike. They all have the same design for their button. This won't do! You won't be able to tell them apart! Of course, you can leave the button appearance as is and click OK. When the macro buttons appear on your toolbar, they look alike, but you can place your mouse over the button and you'll see a descriptive balloon telling you the name of the macro.

Another option is to change the appearance of the buttons. Back in the Customize window, click once on any command that appears in your list on the right side of the window—in this case you'll want to click on one of the macros you've added to the toolbar. Then click the Modify button at the bottom of the list. The Modify Button window appears, as shown in Figure 4-12, displaying nearly 200 button designs from which you can choose. Furthermore, in the Display Name field, you can change the name from something boring, like "PERSONAL.XLSB!FormulaToValue," to "Change formulas to values." Click OK to close the window after you've made your selections.

Customize Your Toolbar for a Particular Workbook

One more thing, before you leave the Excel Options window. Above the list on the right, there is a Customize Quick Access Toolbar drop-down list. By default, any changes you make in this window affect the Quick Access toolbar for all of Excel. But, if you like, you can choose the other option, For *Book1*,

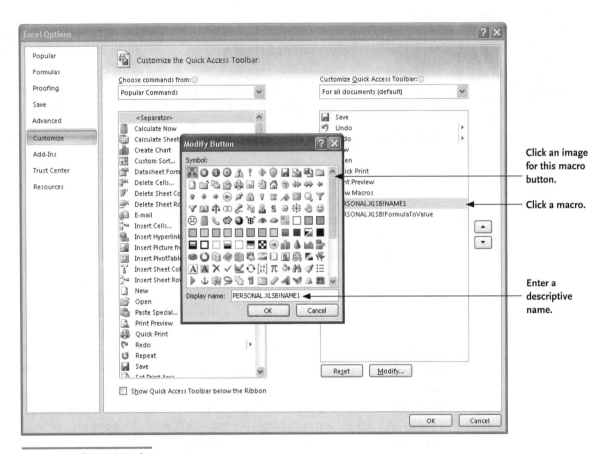

Click an image for this macro button.

Click a macro.

Enter a descriptive name.

Figure 4-12 Customizing the button for a specific macro

where Book1 is the name of your current workbook. You can actually create a Quick Access toolbar that belongs exclusively to one workbook. This is a powerful feature for times when you create macros that belong to just one workbook. Make all the macros easily accessible on the Quick Access toolbar for just that workbook.

Finally, click OK to save your changes. Now you can take a look at your new toolbar, completely customized to make your Excel experiences easier (Figure 4-13).

**Customized Quick
Access Toolbar**

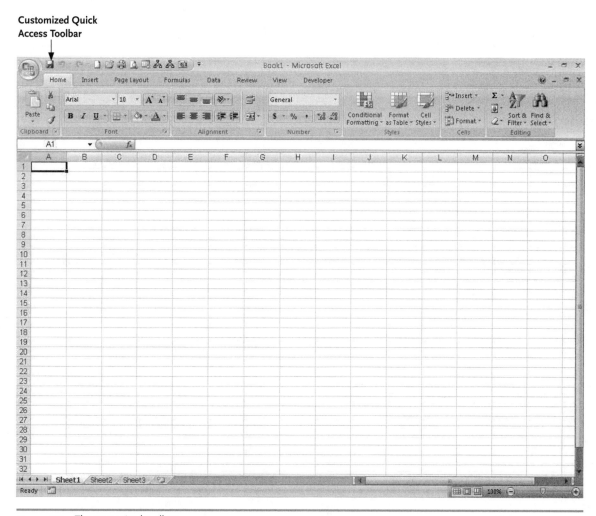

Figure 4-13   The customized toolbar

Understanding Macro Commands

In this chapter you'll see how to write macros rather than simply record them. Recording is an excellent approach, but some things are either easier to do by hand, or just can't be recorded at all. For example, you can display messages to the user on the Excel status bar, as illustrated by an example in Chapter 7. But there is no way to record this action; it must be programmed by hand, by writing code.

And recall that there's also a very common third approach to creating macros: You first record and then use the Editor to modify what you've recorded.

This chapter concludes with an overview of the most commonly used Visual Basic commands, as well as the VB Editor's most important basic features.

Writing Your First Macro

Start Excel running and then press ALT+F11. You now see the VB Editor, as shown in Figure 5-1.

By default three primary windows are displayed in the VB Editor. On the top left is the Project Explorer, which displays the current workbook as well

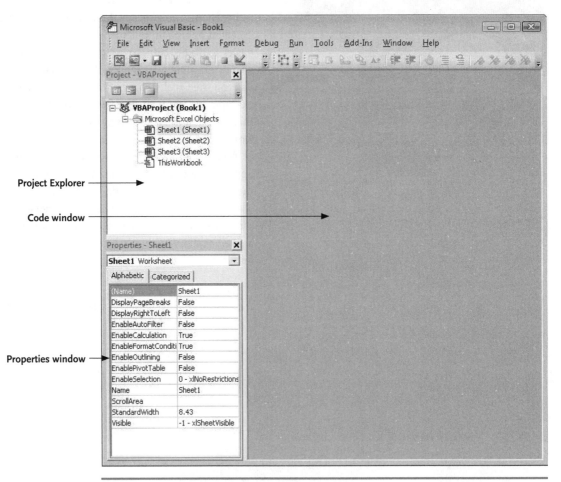

Figure 5-1   The VB Editor, showing the Project Explorer, Properties window, and code window

as all the worksheets it contains. Below this is the Properties window, where the various properties of the currently selected object (in this case Sheet1) are displayed. You can also use this window to edit the properties displayed. For example, you could click on the Name property and change it from *Sheet1* to *Overview* or whatever you wish. When you press ENTER, the name changes both in the Properties window and on the Excel workbook. Note that this is not the same as the (Name) property at the top of the Properties window, which is used internally within the VB Editor. The main point is that the Properties window gives you a convenient way to edit the properties of objects. This window is most useful when creating custom user-interaction windows called UserForms (this topic is covered in Chapter 7).

It's in the code window that you write your macros. You can double-click any sheet or ThisWorkbook in the Project Explorer to open a sheet's code window or the current workbook's code window. The window turns from gray to white, signifying that you can now type programming commands into it.

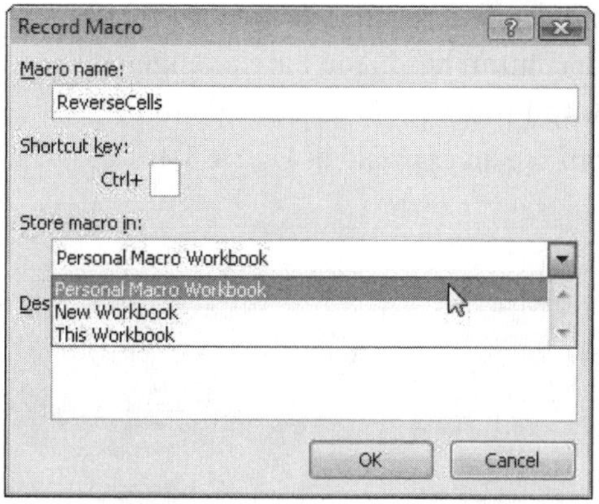

Figure 5-2   Opening the global Personal Macro Workbook in the Project Explorer

WHERE TO STORE YOUR MACROS

Excel allows you to store macros in any worksheet, in the current workbook (*ThisWorkbook* in the Project Explorer), or in modules. (Modules are convenient containers where you can put macros that you want to be accessible from any other location in a project.) In addition, if you write or record a really useful macro that you want to have available always— there's a way to store macros for use with *any* Excel workbook you open, now or in the future. To make a macro available everywhere and always, record it or write it in the special Personal Macro Workbook.

Each time Excel starts, it loads this special workbook (it's the equivalent of Microsoft Office Word 2007's *Normal.dotm* file). Recall that when you click the Record Macro button in Excel, a dialog box opens. In Figure 5-2, you can see in the Store Macro In list box that one option is to store this recorded macro in the global Personal Macro Workbook. Choosing this option adds this workbook and its macros to the Project Explorer. So recording is a quick way to be able to also write macros in the Personal Macro Workbook.

MEMO

Recording macros is a great way to have VBA create code for you. But another shortcut is to look at the VB Editor's Help system to find code examples. You might not need to work from scratch if you can find example code that does what you're after, or at least something similar. Just copy the code from the Help screen, paste it into a code window in the Editor, and then modify it as needed.

Go ahead and add a module now: Choose Insert | Module. Module1 is now added to the Project Explorer, and its code window becomes available to you for programming. Now you can type a macro into the code window, press F5 to test it, and, if necessary, make some modifications so it works just the way you want it to work.

Let's imagine that for your first handcrafted macro, you want to create a vertical label rather than the typical column head. You have a range of numbers, as shown in Figure 5-3, and you want to describe them by displaying a label to their left. You can see an example in Figure 5-4.

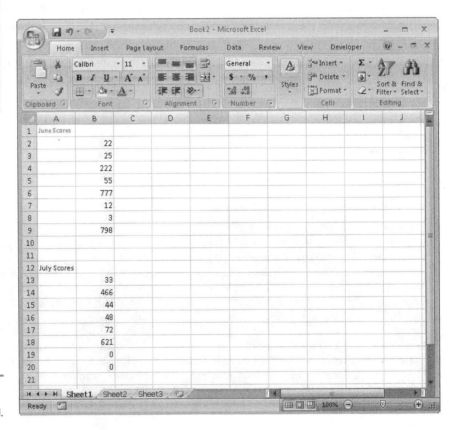

Figure 5-3   You want to create a macro that rotates these labels so they're vertical.

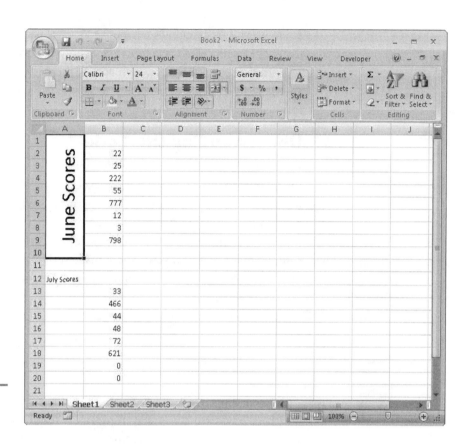

Figure 5-4 This is how you want the sheet to look after your macro executes.

In Module1 in the VB Editor, type this macro:

```
Sub Rotate()
    With Selection
        .MergeCells = True
        .VerticalAlignment = xlCenter
        .Orientation = 90
        .Font.Size = 24
    End With

End Sub
```

Now test it by dragging your mouse to select cells A10 up to A1. Note that this includes, in cell A1, the title June Scores, as shown in Figure 5-3.

With the range selected, switch back to the Editor: Press ALT+F11, click anywhere in your macro, and then press F5 to execute it. You should see the result shown in Figure 5-4.

Understanding the Code

In this macro you don't hard-wire (specify in the code) the cells you want to rotate. Instead, you allow the user to select the range, and then you use the `With Selection` command. This approach is obviously more flexible than a hard-wired range—but of course it demands that the user take extra steps.

The `With` structure—between the `With Selection` and `End With` commands—is handy if you want to make several changes at once to a range or other object. You don't have to repeatedly type the target (`Selection` in this case), like this:

```
Selection.MergeCells = True
Selection.VerticalAlignment = xlCenter
Selection.Orientation = 90
Selection.Font.Size = 24
```

Instead of this redundancy, you put the whole set of changes into a `With` structure. `With` structures also improve the readability of your code because you can see that the list of properties all belong to the same object.

Notice, too, that I've only included the necessary properties in this code: `MergeCells`, `VerticalAlignment`, `Orientation`, and `Font.Size`. It's not necessary to specify additional properties—such as the `FontStyle` or `Underline`—because I'm not changing the font or adding underlining to this text.

Paring Code

The macro in the preceding example could have been recorded rather than written by hand. Let's try that approach to see what happens. When a macro is recorded, *all the properties of the object* are recorded, not just those that are actually needed for the modification under way. This means that even if you're merely changing the orientation, the underline property and many other properties are also included in the recorded macro.

Let's see how this works, and how to fix it. Follow these steps:

1. Select a cell with some text in it.

2. Click the Developer tab on the Ribbon, and then click the Record Macro icon to start the recording process.

3. Right-click that cell and choose Format Cells from the context menu.

4. In the Format Cells dialog box that opens, click the Alignment tab.

5. Drag the Orientation line up to 90 degrees, straight up (or adjust the setting in the Degrees text box).

6. Click OK to close the dialog box.

7. Click the Stop Recording icon in the code section of the Ribbon (the Developer tab must be selected).

8. Press ALT+F11, then open the recorded macro in the VB Editor. You should see code like this:

```
With Selection
        .HorizontalAlignment = xlGeneral
        .VerticalAlignment = xlBottom
        .WrapText = False
        .Orientation = 90
        .AddIndent = False
        .IndentLevel = 0
        .ShrinkToFit = False
        .ReadingOrder = xlContext
        .MergeCells = False
    End With
```

All but one of these properties didn't change—the only property you changed while recording is the `Orientation`. Nevertheless, the recorder took this snapshot of all possible properties.

Many programmers will edit this recorded macro. They'll strip out all but the meaningful properties, the one that changed in this example. This paring out of the unchanged properties makes it easier, later on, to see what this macro is actually doing. And paring also prevents you from accidentally changing important cell properties. The only necessary property change is the orientation, so you can delete all the other lines:

```
With Selection
        .Orientation = 90
End With
```

In our earlier example—showing how to write a macro by hand—we also included some additional property modifications: merging the selected cells, centering the text, and increasing the font size. But you'll recall that indentation, text wrapping, and other properties were left out. They just were not needed, even though the recorder always includes them.

The Elements of Visual Basic

Basic has been around for decades, and for several decades it was the most popular programming language of all. It remains the easiest to use, even though now academic and professional programmers have largely abandoned it in favor of C and its offspring languages.

Why is Basic the easiest? Because its explicit goal is to be as English-like as possible in its diction and syntax. In other words, to end execution of a Basic macro, you use the command `End`. To conclude a `With` structure, you use the command `End With`, and so on. To compare two years' worth of taxes, you use a highly readable Basic "sentence" like this:

```
If TodaysTaxes = LastYearsTaxes Then GoTo NoChange
```

Basic, when possible, tries to use English words and English-like sentences. What could be more sensible or understandable?

Commonly Used Commands

Let's take a look at some of the most commonly used Basic commands, including code examples illustrating how you can employ these commands in your own Excel programming. This overview is by no means

> **Link**   Remember, if you need to accomplish some task not described here, your first step should be to press F1 to open the VB Editor's Help feature. For example, if you want to allow the user to view the file open dialog box that's built into Excel, search VBA Help for something like *file access*. One of the displayed topics is *FileDialog Property*, and it contains an excellent code example you can paste into your macro. If you can't find something in the built-in Help, choose Help | MSDN on the Web, and search there.

exhaustive, but it will introduce you to some important programming concepts, and give you a feel for some of the things you can do by hand-coding macros.

Several important commands are covered elsewhere in this book: message boxes in Chapter 7, variables in Chapter 9, `If...Then` decision-making code in Chapter 10, and `For...Next` looping in Chapter 11. However, what follows in this chapter is a survey of a variety of additional useful VBA commands you should know about, including several sets of commands grouped into categories such as text manipulation, financial calculations, and managing dates and times.

Manipulating Text

When working with text in macros, you are likely to find the set of text manipulation commands quite useful.

For example, sometimes you need to search for a piece of text. Let's say that you ask the

> **Link**   Press F1, then search VBA Help for *String Manipulation Keyword Summary*.

user to type their e-mail address into an input box (described in Chapter 7). One way to make sure they actually entered a proper e-mail address is to search through the string for the @ symbol, which all e-mail addresses have.

To search a string for a substring, you use the `InStr` command, like this:

```
Sub EnterEmail()

    strEmailAddr = InputBox("Please type in your e-mail address")

    test = InStr(strEmailAddr, "@")

    If test = 0 Then
    strEmailAddr = InputBox("Please try again--you did not include
an @ symbol in your e-mail address")

    End If
End Sub
```

When you run this macro, the `InStr` command puts a zero in the variable `test` if no @ symbol was found in the text the user typed into the input box (this text is stored in the variable `strEmailAddr`). So, we can test this by this line of code, and respond with a second request for the address if we find a zero:

```
If test = 0 Then
```

You can probably imagine many situations in programming where it would be useful to parse through a sentence or paragraph to see if a particular word or phrase can be found within that block of text.

VBA includes a large group of text manipulation commands, including the following:

■ The `Mid` command is similar to `InStr`, except that `Mid` returns a substring when you provide the starting position and length of the substring you're after. For example:

```
MsgBox Mid("HellenChange", 2, 5)
```

Results in: ellen.

Get it?

- The `Replace` command is also related to `InStr`, except `Replace` removes a target string and inserts another string in its place, like this:

  ```
  MsgBox Replace("HellenChange", "Hellen", "Dora")
  ```

  Results in: DoraChange

- The `Left` command extracts a substring (there's a `Right` command as well):

  ```
  MsgBox Left ("Miss Petunia", 4)
  ```

  Results in: Miss

  `LCase` changes all the characters to lowercase (there's a `UCase` too):

  ```
  MsgBox LCase("HellenChange")
  ```

  Results in: hellenchange

- The `Format` command has many variations (arguments), and it allows you great freedom in how to display text, dates, financial results, and so on. Press F1 and search Help for *String Manipulation Keyword Summary*.

  `Len` tells you the number of characters (the length of a string):

  ```
  MsgBox Len("HellenChange")
  ```

  Results in: 12

Dates and Times

When you need to employ time or calendar information in a macro, VBA offers you a set of useful commands. Here are some examples:

```
Sub DatesTimes()
    MsgBox Now
    MsgBox Date
    MsgBox Time
    MsgBox Day(Now)
    MsgBox Month(Now)
```

```
        MsgBox Hour(Now)
        MsgBox Minute(Now)

End Sub
```

Link To see the various date and time commands in VBA, press F1, and then search for *Dates and Times Keyword Summary*.

If you run this macro, you'll see a series of time/date data displayed.

VBA even has some commands that perform calculations on time for you, such as the `DateDiff` command, which tells you how many days between today and some future date, like this:

```
Sub DateDifference()
FutureDate = "12/12/2012"
MsgBox "Days from today: " & DateDiff("d", Now, FutureDate)
End Sub
```

Math

All the usual, and some unusual, math operations are available in VBA. You've got + for addition, and – for subtraction, and * for multiplication. The division symbol is a slash (/):

```
MsgBox 5 / 4
```

Results in: 1.25

However, just for good measure, there's another form of division using the backslash (\), called *integer division*. All this does is lop off any decimal point in the answer:

```
MsgBox 5 \ 4
```

Results in: 1

If you ever find a use for that, let me know. Notice that this doesn't *round* the number off; it *lops*. For example 5 \ 3 also results in 1, although if rounded it would be 2. If you really want to round, use the `Round` command, and

84

MEMO

Notice that the `MsgBox` command doesn't require that you use parentheses:

`MsgBox Date`

works just as well as

`MsgBox (Date)`

However, if you're providing an *argument list* (see the briefing in Chapter 7) to a command, you must use parentheses, like this `Now` argument provided to the `Hour` command:

`Hour (Now)`

specify the number of decimal places you're after. Here we want three decimal places:

```
MsgBox Round(5 / 3, 3)
```

Results in: 1.667

Beyond these operators, you'll also find quite a few math functions (search Help for *Math Functions*).

And for all those times when you have to calculate an inverse hyperbolic secant, don't worry, it's there.

Financial Calculations

VBA includes a set of commands that provide some of the features of a financial calculator. Accountants and others involved in the mathematics of business can use these commands to build financial calculating tools. And because macros are extremely flexible, you can customize your calculations far more than is possible with even the most expensive calculators.

Here's an example showing how to figure out the total amount of interest you'll be paying for your home mortgage over the life of the loan. You provide the following information to the macro: *interestrate*, *paymentrange*, *totalperiods*, *presentvalue*, *futurevalue*, *whendue*. Then the IPmt command can give you back the total interest that will be paid over the life of that loan.

Link As with the date commands, you'll also find a generous set of financial commands in VBA. Press F1 and search for *Financial Keyword Summary*. (The word *keyword* is sometimes used as a synonym for the word *command*.)

Here's how it works: The *interestrate* is the interest rate of your loan and should be expressed as the *rate per month* because you pay monthly. Because you'll probably know the interest in terms of an annual rate, divide by 12. Our rate is 6 percent, so the *rate* figure should be .06 (the interest rate) / 12 (the months in a year). The resulting rate is .005. We'll use the name *irate* for interest rate variable in this command because VBA already has

85

a command called `Rate` (described later in this section). As you'll see in Chapter 9, you can't name a variable using a word that VBA already uses for one of its built-in commands.

The *paymentrange* is how much of the total time of the loan you want to figure the interest for. We'll use a `For...Next` loop for this calculation, so the *paymentrange* variable will change dynamically when we're calculating, moving us through the entire life of the loan.

The *totalperiods* is the number of times you pay the mortgage over the life of the loan. Ours is a 15-year mortgage, and we pay monthly. So the *totalperiods* is 15 * 12 (which results in 180).

The *presentvalue* means the total amount you're borrowing. Our house cost $50,000 (it's a total fixer-upper), but you should express this number as a negative, so it's –50000.

The *futurevalue* is the cash balance you want to have at the end of the mortgage. For loans, *futurevalue* is zero.

The *whendue* value is either 1 or 0. It's 1 if payments are due at the beginning of each month; it's 0 if payments are due at the end of each month. We pay at the end, so *whendue* is 0.

Now that we've answered these questions, we can use the following macro to calculate the interest:

```
Private Sub Interest()

irate = 0.005
totalperiods = 180
presentvalue = -50000
futurevalue = 0
whendue = 0
For paymentrange = 1 To totalperiods
Tempinterest = IPmt(irate, paymentrange, totalperiods,
presentvalue, futurevalue, hendue)
Totalinterest = Totalinterest + Tempinterest
Next paymentrange
MsgBox "The total that you'll pay for this loan is: " &
Format(Totalinterest + Abs(presentvalue), "###,###,##0.00")
```

```
MsgBox "Of that, the interest is: " & Format(Totalinterest,
"###,###,##0.00")
End Sub
```

When you execute this macro, it tells you that the total that you'll pay for this loan is $75,947.11. And of that, $25,947.11 is interest.

Don't be alarmed by this code. The `Format` command, for example, is easy to understand when you look it up in VBA Help. Just click the word `Format` in your macro code to put the blinking insertion cursor in it, then press F1 and you'll see many dozens of examples of its use.

As for understanding how to employ the various financial commands in VBA, you'll find plenty of code examples for them as well.

Error

You sometimes want to put an *error handler* in your macros. This way, if something goes wrong, your macro doesn't just mysteriously stop executing, or otherwise frighten the user. Instead, you can display a message explaining what happened and what the user can do about it.

Here is a typical error-handling structure. First, you tell VBA where to go—a place in the macro where you've put the label `Showit`—if an error occurs:

```
On Error GoTo Showit
```

You can use any name you want instead of `Showit`; it's just a target where the macro starts executing code if an error happens.

Next, we have a line that *induces* a fake error (`Error 70`) just so we can test the error handler. This line would be replaced by the actual code in your macro.

Typically an `Exit Sub` command appears just above any error handler code. This prevents the program from reaching the handler unless an error actually sends us to the handler.

Then the Showit section prints the error message, in this case *Permission Denied* (because we induced error #70). Finally, the VB command Resume Next is used to send VB back up to the line *following* the On Error GoTo:

```
Sub Errors ()
On Error GoTo Showit
Error 70

Exit Sub
Showit:
        MsgBox Error(Err)
        Resume Next
End Sub
```

This code displays the error description in a message box to the user. However, before you finish your macro and give it to others, you'll probably want to replace that built-in message with a more helpful, more descriptive message of your own, such as:

```
MsgBox ("See the network administrator. You don't have
security clearance to do this.")
```

GETTING ACQUAINTED WITH THE VB EDITOR

Developed during decades of user feedback, focus groups, and refinement, the VB Editor is a polished gem. No matter how many years you spend, or how deeply you go into VBA programming, I doubt you'll ever find yourself wishing for a particular feature. It's filled with everything a programmer needs.

Beginners, however, can get a head start by knowing about several important features in advance. No point stumbling on them. I'll just tell you the essentials in this briefing.

The File and Edit Menus

The File and Edit menus contain most of the usual tools you'd find in a word processor. And any programmer's editor is a word processor, albeit highly specialized. The Edit menu includes the usual find, cut, copy, paste, and other text manipulation capabilities, but it also has options specific to programming. Click your mouse on a command such as MsgBox in the code editor, to select it, and then try choosing Edit | Quick to see the syntax for this command.

GETTING ACQUAINTED WITH THE VB EDITOR (CONT.)

The View Menu

On the View menu you can choose to display the important Project Explorer or Properties window, if you've previously closed them. You can also display the Toolbox if you're working on a UserForm (see Chapter 7).

The Format Menu

The Format menu contains a variety of options, most useful when prettying up a UserForm.

The Debug Menu

On the Debug menu, you'll find all kinds of useful features that can help you track down elusive errors in your code.

The Run Menu

On the Run menu, the most useful option here for beginners is the Run | Reset option. Click that if you ever see the message shown in the illustration.

Beginners are baffled by this error message. It's displayed when you run a macro that has an error in it, and the VB Editor automatically enters "break mode," a special condition where execution of the macro is stopped. However, something else happens too: Further execution of that macro or any other macro is now not possible in this mode (programmers use a variety of the tools on the Debug menu during break mode). But you'll often want to get out of this break mode and back to normal. To exit from break mode, choose Run | Reset.

That's it. I've not covered every option, or, indeed, every menu. Some are self-explanatory, like the Window | Cascade option. If you don't know what this means in a word processor, try it and see.

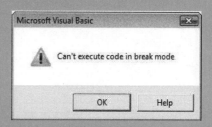

Using Visual Basic Subroutines and Creating Functions

A subroutine is like a little macro that operates within a larger macro. The subroutine code resides within the main macro. When a macro calls a subroutine, the execution of the macro is diverted to the subroutine area of the macro.

One common use for subroutines is to break up a complex macro into smaller parts. Also, subroutines can be useful in macros that provide the user with a choice. If you select choice A, the macro diverts to the A subroutine. Select choice B and the B subroutine is called into action. For example, let's say you have defined two print areas on the screen. The macro asks the user to indicate which print area should be printed. Choosing print area 1 causes the macro to divert to the Print1 subroutine. Choosing print area 2 causes the macro to divert to the Print2 subroutine. In this scenario, when the print job has been completed or has been canceled, macro execution ends. Choosing a third option, Cancel, causes the macro to proceed without printing, or, in this case, to end.

Alternatively, if a function within your macro produces one set of results, one subroutine runs; another set of results causes a different subroutine to run. For example, the macro examines a cell containing a number. If the number is less than 1,000, the cell is rounded up to 1,000. If the number is greater than 1,000, there is no change to the cell contents.

Creating a Subroutine

Because a subroutine runs within an existing macro, there needs to be a way to set the subroutine commands apart from the rest of the macro. This is done by assigning a name to the subroutine. The macro then calls the subroutine by its name with the GoTo command. The subroutine itself begins with its name as the first line, followed by the command lines associated with that subroutine, and the subroutine ends with an End command. Alternatively, you can call the subroutine with the GoSub command. When you use GoSub, operation returns to the jump-off point in the macro when the subroutine is finished.

Here's an example. Say you've designated two areas of your worksheet as different print areas, and you've assigned range names to these areas, PrintArea1 and PrintArea2. You want to create a macro that asks the user if he wants to print what he knows as Report 1 (which equates to PrintArea1) or Report 2 (which equates to PrintArea2). His answer is stored in the macro as 1 or 2. If he answers 1, the macro executes a subroutine called Print1. If he answers 2, the macro executes a subroutine called Print2. If the user answers something other than 1 or 2, the question appears again and he has another chance to answer. The question itself is treated as a subroutine as well, so that it can be recalled if necessary.

Naming a Subroutine

Designate the name of a subroutine by entering the name you want, followed by a colon. Use only one word for the subroutine name. For this example, the three subroutines will be called:

Answer:

Print1:

Print2:

These names are referred to as labels.

Calling the Subroutines

The first subroutine required for this macro performs the task of asking the user a question. This code is quite simple—it utilizes the concept of an input box with a field available for the user to enter his answer. Input boxes are discussed in more detail in Chapter 7. For now, we'll just use the InputBox code with just a minimal description. The code begins with a variable that gets assigned the value of the InputBox. So whatever the user enters as his answer (in this case 1 or 2), that value gets assigned to the variable, which we will call Report. Here's the line of code:

```
Report = InputBox("Enter 1 to print Report 1; Enter 2 to
print Report 2")
```

The information that appears in the quotation marks is the text that appears in the input box that the user will see. His entry of 1 or 2 becomes the value of the variable, Report.

Once Report has a value, the macro can proceed by determining which subroutine to run, based on the value of Report.

Your macro is going to state that, if the value of Report is 1, then subroutine Print1 will execute. If the value of Report is 2, subroutine Print2 will execute. If Report has any other value, the question will reappear. The code is quite straightforward:

```
If Report = 1 Then
      GoTo Print1
ElseIf Report = 2 Then
      GoTo Print2
Else
      GoTo Question
End If
```

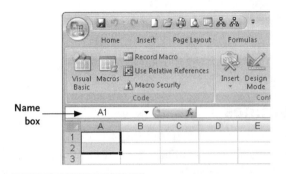

Name box

Figure 6-1 Assign range names to print areas.

Using the concept of an `If/Then/Else` command, the macro enables the user to make an intelligent choice. We'll learn more about `If/Then/Else` routines in Chapter 10, but as you can see, the concept is quite easy to understand.

Writing the Subroutines

The subroutines themselves in this example are VBA print commands. You can turn on your macro recorder and record yourself printing a print area in order to harvest the code. Before recording the macro, name the print areas PrintArea1 and PrintArea2 (select the area, right-click, and choose Name). Then, with the macro recorder on, click the down arrow in the Name box (see Figure 6-1), choose PrintArea1 to select the area, and then choose File | Print | Selection | OK. Turn off the recorder, and you will find this code in your VB Editor:

```
Application.Goto Reference:="PrintArea1"
ExecuteExcel4Macro "PRINT(1,,,1,,,,,,,,1,,,TRUE,,FALSE)"
```

This is all the code you need for your subroutine, thus the Print1 subroutine will look like this:

```
Print1:
    Application.Goto Reference:="PrintArea1"
    ExecuteExcel4Macro "PRINT(1,,,1,,,,,,,,1,,,TRUE,,FALSE)"
    End
```

The Print2 subroutine will be identical to the Print1 subroutine, except for the substitution of Print2 and PrintArea2. The last subroutine we need to create to make this work is the Question area of the macro, which utilizes the `InputBox` code discussed previously, as well as the `If/Then/Else` statement. First the macro will ask the user the question, and then it executes the proper print commands:

```
Sub SpecialPrint()
Question:
```

```
Report = InputBox("Enter 1 to print Report 1; Enter 2 to print
Report 2")
If Report = 1 Then
      GoTo Print1
ElseIf Report = 2 Then
      GoTo Print2
Else
      GoTo Question
End If
Print1:
      Application.Goto Reference:="PrintArea1"
      ExecuteExcel4Macro "PRINT(1,,,1,,,,,,,,1,,,TRUE,,FALSE)"
      End
Print2:
      Application.Goto Reference:="PrintArea2"
      ExecuteExcel4Macro "PRINT(1,,,1,,,,,,,,1,,,TRUE,,FALSE)"
      End
End sub
```

Figure 6-2 shows how the operating macro looks to the user.

If you want to really get creative and make this macro more easily accessible to the user, so that he doesn't have to hunt for it on the

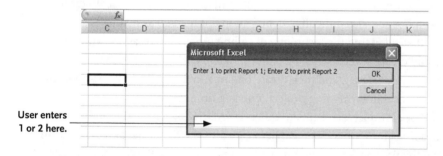

User enters 1 or 2 here.

Figure 6-2   Calling a subroutine

Macros menu, you can place the order for the macro in a button and place that button on the actual worksheet. Chapter 12 discusses how this process works.

Running Macros as Subroutines

You've seen how we can insert subroutines into a macro and call on these bits of code as necessary. You can also have a macro call another macro, as if it is a subroutine, because technically, all macros are actually subprocedures, hence the use of the Sub, End Sub commands to start and end each macro.

Once a macro is created, its name serves as a command. Thus the macro GetMyName can be designed to call the NAME1 macro created in Chapter 1:

```
Sub GetMyName()
NAME1
End Sub
```

While this particular example might seem useless—creating a new macro for the purposes of calling an existing macro—you might be able to visualize the usefulness of this process when thinking about creating many different macros and calling them as necessary in the course of a new macro. For example, in Chapter 1 we created a macro that applied several different formatting changes to a worksheet. It's quite possible that placing so many recorded commands in a single macro might overwhelm the novice macro programmer, particularly if the person recording the commands made mistakes and then corrected them along the way, or chose additional formatting features to add. The macro can grow large and be both difficult to decipher and also difficult to debug should it not run as planned.

Instead, using the technique of calling other macros as shown here, you could create several small formatting macros, make sure each does its own task appropriately, and then create one macro that calls on the various pieces of the overall formatting project, one at a time.

For example, take a macro called HEADINGS that creates and formats the headings for a worksheet, a macro called COLUMNS that assigns column width and number formatting codes, a macro called ROWS that formats the row titles, and a macro called TOTALS that places totals at the bottom of each column of numbers. All four macros could be combined in one MonthlyReportSetup macro like this:

```
Sub MonthlyReportSetup
HEADINGS
COLUMNGS
ROWS
TOTALS
End Sub
```

We'll take a look at formatting macros in greater depth in Chapter 8 and will discuss this process of running macros as subroutines at that time.

Using skills you will learn in Chapter 7, you can even customize the formatting further, by asking the user with the help of an input box which formatting features he would like to utilize, and then use subroutines to call the various formatting macros as needed.

Creating a Customized Function

Similar to creating macros, you can use the VB Editor to create your own customized functions. Functions you create are added to the Excel function list, so they can be called as easily as the AVERAGE or the COUNT function. This is a great time-saver if you need to execute complicated calculations. Not only can you condense your calculations into one simple function, but this function can be made available to all of your other Excel worksheets. Another use for customized functions is as a means of protecting the details of a calculation.

Use a Function to Make a Complicated Calculation Easy

Suppose you need to calculate corporate income tax on a regular basis. The corporate income tax is calculated at different levels, with the tax rate changing as the tax-paying corporation's income increases. So, for example, a corporation with taxable income of $100,000 pays 15 percent tax on the first $50,000, 25 percent tax on the next $25,000, and 34 percent on the balance. The corporate tax rates for 2008 are shown in Table 6-1.

It's possible to write a nested IF formula that will calculate this tax, no matter what the level of income is, but there's no doubt that will be a complicated formula and cumbersome to re-create

Taxable Income		
Over	Not Over	Tax Rate
$ 0	$ 50,000	15%
50,000	75,000	25%
75,000	100,000	34%
100,000	335,000	39%
335,000	10,000,000	34%
10,000,000	15,000,000	35%
15,000,000	18,333,333	38%
18,333,333	....	35%

Table 6-1   2008 U.S. Corporate Income Tax Rates

if you have to use the formula frequently. Instead, you can create a function that does the calculation for you. Not only will you never have to worry about creating the formula again, but you can share the function with anyone else who needs to calculate corporate tax.

To create the new function, which we'll call `CorpTax`, open the VB Editor. We'll make this accessible to all worksheets, so open a new module in the Personal Macro Workbook (click on the Personal Project, and then choose Insert | Module).

The first line of a function is different from that of a macro, even though the creation process is basically the same. Instead of `Sub macroname`, you'll enter `Function functionname`, or in this case:

```
Function CorpTax
```

In addition, as you may recall, macro names are followed by a set of parentheses. We need that for the function name as well. In this case, we're going to place a word inside the parentheses: Income. *Income* will be the variable that is required by this function—the function performs calculations on the Income amount. Placing Income in the parentheses will make this function ask us to identify which cell contains the income for the purposes of the CorpTax calculations. So the complete first line of our function will be

```
Function CorpTax(Income)
```

Now we're ready to enter the code for this function. We're going to use the VBA `Select Case` statement, a procedure that is similar to the `IF` statement. The `Select Case` structure allows you to order an action to be performed only if a certain condition is met. In this situation, we'll set the `Case` to be equal to the amount specified as `Income`. Once we establish that we're working with the Income amount, we can list the criteria set forth in the tax schedule at Table 6-1. Here's how it looks:

```
Function CorpTax(Income)
Select Case Income
Case Is > 18333333: CorpTax = Income * 0.35
```

MEMO

The word `Function` tells Excel that this is a function. Calling this a function instead of a macro enables Excel to add the function to the master function list.

MEMO

If you're confused about how we decide where the parentheses go in the formulas that appear in this function, see the section "Arithmetic Operators in Order of Precedence" in Chapter 9.

```
Case Is > 15000000: CorpTax = 515000 + (Income - 15000000) * 0.38
Case Is > 10000000: CorpTax = 3400000 + (Income - 10000000) * 0.35
Case Is > 335000: CorpTax = 113900 + (Income - 335000) * 0.34
Case Is > 100000: CorpTax = 22250 + (Income - 100000) * 0.39
Case Is > 75000: CorpTax = 13750 + (Income - 75000) * 0.34
Case Is > 50000: CorpTax = 7500 + (Income - 1500) * 0.25
Case Is > 0: CorpTax = Income * 0.15
End Select
End Function
```

The way this case procedure works is that, as soon as the case criterion is met, the calculation is performed, and the function stops. If the corporation's income is $15,000,001, the first case criterion will be examined, and since the income is not > $18,333,333, this will be rejected and the function moves to the second criterion. Because this criterion applies, the calculation is performed at this point in the function, and the remaining case options are ignored. If the corporation's income is $10,000, the function will proceed through each possible scenario, rejecting each one, until the final scenario, Case Is > 0, is met, and the tax is calculated.

Once the function is entered into the VB Editor, choose File | Save PERSONAL.XLSB, and you're ready to test this function.

Back in the worksheet, enter some numbers in a column. These numbers represent the taxable income of some corporations. Follow these steps to run your new function:

THE EASY WAY

Save your changes in the VB Editor quickly by pressing CTRL+S.

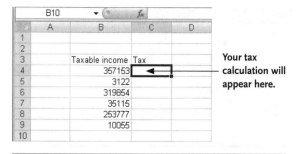

Your tax calculation will appear here.

Figure 6-3   Taxable income in need of tax calculation

1. Click in the cell where you want the first tax calculation to appear (see Figure 6-3).

2. Click the Formulas tab.

3. Click the Insert Function button on the ribbon.

4. In the Insert Function dialog box (see Figure 6-4), select the All category.

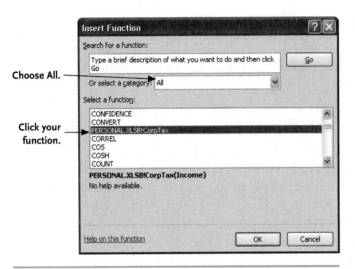

Choose All.

Click your function.

Figure 6-4   Finding your new function

5. Scroll through the alphabetical list until you find your CorpTax function. It will be alphabetized under "C" but will appear as PERSONAL.XLSB!CorpTax.

6. Click OK.

7. Click the cell identifier box in the Function Arguments window and then click on the cell containing the taxable income, and click the red button to return to the Function Arguments window. Alternatively, you can enter the cell reference for the taxable income cell in the Income field of the Function Arguments window. Notice that the tax calculation now appears in this window. See Figure 6-5.

100

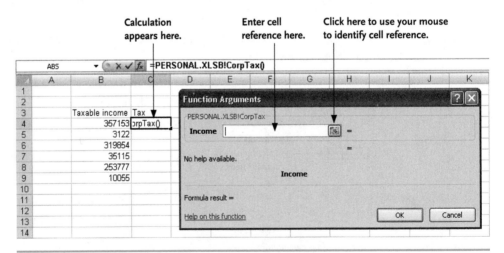

Calculation appears here.

Enter cell reference here.

Click here to use your mouse to identify cell reference.

Figure 6-5   Using the CorpTax function

MEMO

Remember that your new function is actually called PERSONAL .XLSB!CorpTax. If you try to enter CorpTax as a function name in your worksheet, you will get an error message.

8. Click OK to place the tax calculation on your worksheet.

9. Note that you now can copy this formula to other cells in your worksheet without having to open the Insert Function window again.

Use a Customized Function to Hide Sensitive Data

Rather than planning a formula on a worksheet where everyone can see it, you can create a function that lives in the VB Editor, where only authorized eyes can view the calculation process. For example, say it's time to calculate bonuses for employees and the bonus calculation is a secret formula.

We'll start with a spreadsheet that lists employees and the quarterly revenue that they generated. In this fictitious company, second-quarter sales are typically quite high due to the seasonal nature of the business. So the company owners want to reward their salespeople with a higher bonus for sales that exceed quota in quarters 1, 3, and 4, and a lower bonus in quarter 2. Here's the secret formula:

Q1 sales * .1%
Q2 sales * .05%
Q3 sales * .08%
Q4 sales * .075%

Here's the function that the company owners want to create:

```
Function Bonus (Q1, Q2, Q3, Q4)
Bonus = Q1 * .001 + Q2 * .0005 + Q3 * .0008 + Q4 * .00075
End Function
```

When this function is entered into a module in the Personal Macro Workbook and saved, it joins the other functions on the function list and is accessible by any macro, but without the calculation formula revealed.

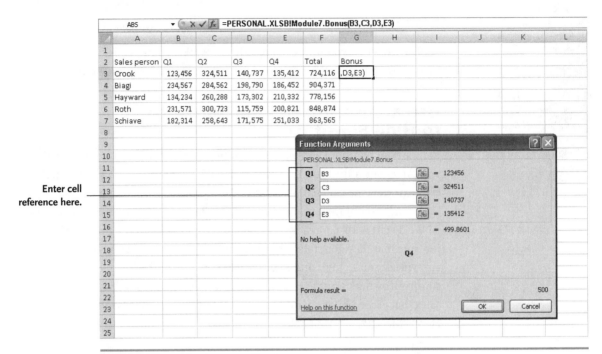

Figure 6-6   Enter cell references as function arguments.

No calculation information appears.

Figure 6-7   Hiding calculation details in functions

Apply the function by clicking in the cell where you want the bonus to appear, choosing Bonus from the Function list (see Figure 6-6), and entering the cell references for the Q1, Q2, Q3, and Q4 amounts. Once one bonus is entered, the function can be copied into other cells.

You'll notice that the Formula bar shows only the name of the function and the cell references, but no calculation information. See Figure 6-7.

Creating Interactive Macros

As you've seen in earlier chapters, many macros can run all by themselves, without requiring any input from the user. For example, if you create a macro that enters your initials in the upper-left cell, it might look like this:

```
Sub InsertInitials()
    Range("A1").Select
    ActiveCell.FormulaR1C1 = "GP"
End Sub
```

Other macros, though, require that you halt macro execution and ask the user for some input. Maybe you want the user to type in their initials? It's OK to *hard-code* the initials if you're the only person who will be using this macro. But if you want the macro to be useful to others, you have to let them enter their initials. This means accepting input from the user while the macro is running. One way to accept input from the user while a macro executes is to display an input box to the user.

USING ARGUMENTS

In programming, an *argument* is some data that you supply to a command such as the `InputBox` command. In VBA, these data are enclosed in parentheses. Here is the complete syntax for the `InputBox` command in VBA:

```
InputBox(Prompt, Title, Default, Left,
Top, HelpFile, HelpContextID, Type)
```

Each item within the parentheses is an argument. But most arguments are optional—you can omit them, and often you simply don't need them, which is why they're optional in the first place. The only *required* argument for an input box is the `Prompt`, which is a brief label that appears just above the text box where users type in their data. This caption tells the user what to type in. So, the programming that displays the simplest kind of input box uses only one argument, the `Prompt` argument, like this:

```
x = InputBox("Please enter your
initials")
```

Figure 7-1 illustrates this input box. The user sees the descriptive prompt and can type whatever they wish in the text box.

If you provide no `Title` argument, the title bar of the input box displays *Microsoft Excel*. However, you can, if you wish, provide your own argument for the title, like this:

```
x = InputBox("Please enter your
initials", "Enter Initials")
```

Figure 7-2 illustrates the result of adding an optional title.

The third argument, `Default`, is also optional, but can be useful in some situations. Let's say that you have an idea what information the user will type in. You can save the user time by displaying that information as the default in the text box. That way, the user doesn't have to type anything in if your default is correct. They merely have to press ENTER, or click the OK button. However, the user is also free to replace your default text with his or her own input, if necessary. Here's how to add a default argument to the `InputBox` command:

```
x = InputBox("Please enter your
initials", "Enter Initials", "GP")
```

Notice in Figure 7-3 that the *GP* default data is automatically selected (highlighted) so the user can just type in some new data if necessary. If this default data were not selected, the user would have to select it to replace it.

As you can see, each argument that you add inside the parentheses is separated from the other arguments by commas. And it *is* necessary that you keep these arguments in the proper order. In this case, the order is: `Prompt`, `Title`, `Default`, and so on. This order is how VBA knows which argument is which, and doesn't confuse, for example, the title with the prompt. Even optional arguments must be included (or commas indicating that they are missing) if subsequent arguments are used. For example, if you want to include a default, but omit the title, you must still use the proper number of commas, like this:

```
x = InputBox("Please enter your
initials", , "GP")
```

MEMO

The term *hard-coded* or *hard-wired* in programming means that something is included in the macro that never changes. In the previous example, the initials *GP* are inserted into the upper-left cell. It's hard-wired because they're my initials. However, a more flexible approach is sometimes required. Instead of supplying the data *GP* in your macro, you allow the user to supply their own initials. You get this data by using an input box or some other kind of "control" such as a message box, or, as you'll see later in this chapter, a list box.

The user enters initials in the input filed.

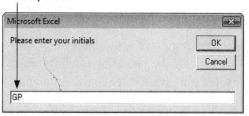

Figure 7-1   The simplest kind of input box

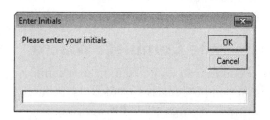

Figure 7-2   You can add an optional title to your input box.

Figure 7-3   You can supply default information that the user is free to either accept or replace.

An input box is displayed to the user by employing the `InputBox` command. But before you can effectively use commands like `InputBox`, you need to understand the concept of *arguments* in programming. An `InputBox`, like many other objects, has a list of arguments.

Note that *optional* arguments are enclosed in brackets; required arguments, such as `Prompt` in Figure 7-4, are not thus enclosed.

```
inputbox
InputBox(Prompt, [Title], [Default], [XPos], [YPos], [HelpFile], [Context]) As String
```

Figure 7-4   The Auto Quick Info feature shows you the list of arguments at a glance.

Understanding How the Input Box Works

You might have wondered about the X in the code examples above. This is a *variable*, and we'll explore this essential programming tool in depth in Chapter 9. For now, it's enough to understand that when the user types in some data, then clicks the OK button (or presses ENTER) to close the input box, the X contains the data the user typed in. So you can then use X in your macro later to retrieve the data.

Writing the Complete Macro

In this example, you want to put the user's initials in the upper-left cell. Here's the complete macro that displays the input box and then puts whatever the user types into that cell in the worksheet:

```
Sub GetInitials()
    x = InputBox("Please enter your initials", "Enter Initials")

    Range("A1").Select
    ActiveCell.FormulaR1C1 = x
End Sub
```

This code first displays an input box to the user, and when the user closes this box, whatever the user typed into the input box's text box is now contained in the variable X.

Writing and Testing Input Box Code

It's time for you to type in the code that displays an input box, then test that code in the VB Editor. Follow these steps:

1. With Excel running and a worksheet visible, press ALT+F11.

2. This opens the VB Editor so you can write a macro.

3. In the VB Editor, choose Insert | Module.

MEMO

If the user doesn't type anything into the input box, the variable X will contain nothing. Sometimes it's useful to test whether the user typed nothing, and you can do that by seeing if $X = ""$ (an empty string), like this:
`If x = "" Then`
`Exit Sub`
This code causes the macro to stop executing (to exit the subroutine) if the user typed nothing into the input box. In other words, any programming code below this line will be ignored by VBA if the user left the text box blank. We use an `If...Then` structure (described in detail in Chapter 10) to test the value in the variable X.

A new macro container opens (a module can contain multiple macros). The Editor displays a blank window on the right (the code window) and highlights the newly created module in the Project Explorer (if you have that explorer visible) as shown on the left in Figure 7-5.

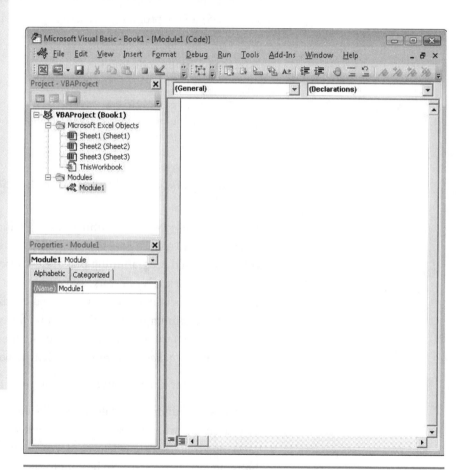

Figure 7-5   Write or modify macros in the code window on the right in the VB Editor.

The new module will be called Module1 if this is the first module you've added to this project. The next module is named by default Module2, and so on. However, you can always click a module's name in the Project Explorer to select that module, and then change its Name property in the Properties window (shown in the lower left in Figure 7-5). Many programmers like to give their modules descriptive names, such as *TaxMacros* or *InventoryMacros*.

4. Type the following code into the code module:

```
Sub GetInitials()
    Dim strInitials As String
    strInitials = InputBox("Please enter your
initials", "Enter Initials")

    Range("A1").Select
    ActiveCell.FormulaR1C1 = strInitials
End Sub
```

Notice that I used the Dim command here to formally declare a variable—strInitials—that will hold the user's input. This is considered good programming practice because declaring variables can avoid some kinds of errors, and also makes the code somewhat easier to understand and read. I also used another common convention, naming the variable with a prefix, str, identifying it as a string (text) variable type. Finally, using the word *Initials* in the variable name makes it easier to see what purpose the variable serves.

5. Finally, test your newly written macro by pressing F5.

This tells the Editor to execute the macro, and also hides the Editor so you can see what happens in the current worksheet. Note that pressing F5 will execute whatever macro currently displays the blinking insertion cursor. So be sure to click within the macro's code to put the cursor in it before pressing F5.

Message Boxes: Simpler Communication with the User

If you want to display a message to the user about something while a macro runs—but don't need any input from the user—use a message box. This control is similar to an input box, but a message box has no text box into which the user can type. And, in its simplest form, a message box has only a single button, OK, that the user clicks after reading whatever the message box says. In the MsgBox command, you type the message as the Prompt argument, and that's the only required argument. The command for creating a message box looks like an abbreviation: MsgBox.

```
MsgBox ("Cells have been reformatted.")
```

When this message is displayed (see Figure 7-6), users can't provide your macro with any input. All they can do is click OK or press ENTER to close the message box.

Using Message Box Buttons for Feedback

You can, however, use a message box to send back limited information from the user to your macro. To do this, you can display various sets of built-in buttons. Here's the formal syntax for the arguments that you can provide to a message box:

```
MsgBox(prompt[, buttons] [, title] [, helpfile, context])
```

Notice that the Prompt is the only argument that is required. However, the Buttons argument can be optionally included to display buttons other than the default OK button. The five optional sets of buttons for a message box are shown in Table 7-1.

All you have to do to display an optional set of buttons is to provide the Value number as the Buttons argument. Say, for example, that you

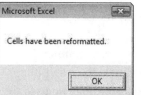

Figure 7-6   A simple message box merely displays information to the user, but can't send any user input back to the macro.

Constant	Value	Description
vbOKCancel	1	Displays OK and Cancel buttons.
vbAbortRetryIgnore	2	Displays Abort, Retry, and Ignore buttons.
vbYesNoCancel	3	Displays Yes, No, and Cancel buttons.
vbYesNo	4	Displays Yes and No buttons.
vbRetryCancel	5	Displays Retry and Cancel buttons.

Table 7-1   Optional Buttons That Can Be Displayed in a Message Box

wanted to display the common Yes, No, and Cancel buttons. You would use the value **3** as your `Buttons` argument, as illustrated in the following code:

```
x = MsgBox("Do you want to continue?", 3)
```

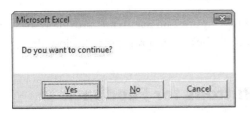

Figure 7-7   This message box provides user feedback to your macro, based on which button is clicked.

Execute this code and you'll see the message box displayed in Figure 7-7.

Notice that when you use the `Buttons` argument, you must provide a variable that will hold the result (the user's choice of buttons). In our code example, we used the variable X. After the user clicks a button, X contains one of the values shown in Table 7-2.

Here's a complete macro illustrating how to use buttons in your code:

Constant	Value	Description
vbOK	1	OK
vbCancel	2	Cancel
vbAbort	3	Abort
vbRetry	4	Retry
vbIgnore	5	Ignore
vbYes	6	Yes
vbNo	7	No

Table 7-2   Returned Values for MsgBox Button Clicks

```
Sub Message()
x = MsgBox("Do you want to continue?", 3)
If x = 7 Then Exit Sub
MsgBox ("OK, we'll continue with this macro.")
End Sub
```

When this macro executes, it displays a message box with Yes, No, and Cancel buttons. We get the user's response in the variable X. That response can be 6, 7, or 2, based on whether the user clicks the Yes, No, or Cancel button respectively.

110

THE EASY WAY

Some programmers prefer to use *built-in constants* rather than *values* when performing such tasks as specifying arguments or testing variables. Sometimes when you look at an argument list in the VBA Help system, you'll see tables like Table 7-1 or 7-2. When you write your macro you can use either the value (such as *2*) or the constant (a descriptive word, like vbCancel). Here's how the previous example code would look if you chose to use the constants:

```
Sub Message()

x = MsgBox("Do
you want to
continue?",
vbYesNoCancel)

If x = vbNo
Then Exit Sub

MsgBox ("OK,
we'll continue
with this
macro.")

End Sub
```

In this case, we use an If...Then structure to test the value in X. If the value is 7, the user responded by clicking No when asked if they wanted to continue, so we exit the subroutine (Exit Sub) and thereby stop the macro from running. But if they clicked the Yes or Cancel buttons, the subroutine is not exited; the rest of the macro executes, and another message box is displayed.

Using the Status Bar for More Subtle Feedback

Input boxes and message boxes are excellent ways to communicate between your macro and the user. But they do have one potential drawback: *they stop your macro in its tracks,* just like a salesman who puts his foot in your door.

You can't continue executing a macro until the input box or message box is closed. It sits there and demands notice. Often this is desirable. Your macro wants the user to be sure to see a message, or some information must be supplied by the user. But what about situations where you want to display information that the user can optionally ignore? Take the example earlier in this chapter. It used a message box to tell the user that cells have been reformatted. Generally, the user knows that they've just reformatted cells, so there's no need to stop everything to display a message box telling them this. However, they might want to sometimes check to see if cells have been reformatted.

A solution is to display this kind of optional information on the status bar at the bottom of the Excel window. The information will be visible to the user, but it won't halt execution like a message box does. Here's an example showing how to use the StatusBar object in your code to display a message:

```
Sub StatusBarMessage()
Application.StatusBar = "Cells have been formatted..."
End Sub
```

Try this little macro and see how it works. To erase the contents of the status bar, use this code:

```
Application.StatusBar = ""
```

Creating Custom Dialogs

You now know how to use various sets of buttons to provide the user with a way of communicating simple information to your macro—such as cancel, ignore, or retry. But you sometimes want to allow the user to select from a larger or more varied group of options. For example, rather than forcing the user to type in the name of a state, you can provide a list of all the states, from Alabama to Wyoming.

Or you may need to get extensive or complex information from the user. You might need to display a form for them to fill in. To do this, you can create your own custom dialog box. It's not an input box or message box, but instead something you craft to suit special user-interaction requirements. The VB Editor has sophisticated tools that allow you to design many kinds of forms the user can fill in. These are called UserForms. They can be small, like input boxes, or they can fill the screen. UserForms allow you great freedom in how you design them and what controls you put on them.

Offering the User a List of Options

To see how to work with UserForms, let's design one now. You will add a ListBox to a form, and also add Cancel and OK buttons, so the user has a way of closing your dialog box (a UserForm, when displayed to the user, is usually called a dialog box).

In this example, you want to display a list of options to the user. Let's assume that you regularly need to change the font size in various cells to small, medium, or large. You want to display a dialog box that the user can click to select between these options.

To add a UserForm to your project, follow these steps:

1. Start Excel running and press ALT+F11 to open the VB Editor.

2. Choose Insert | UserForm.

    You now see the Editor looking like Figure 7-8—with a new, blank form in the right window (this is called the design window when you're building a form). You also see the Toolbox on the left side, containing the various controls you can add to the form. If you don't see the Toolbox, choose View | Toolbox.

3. Move your mouse pointer around the Toolbox. Each time you pause the mouse on an icon, a description of that icon appears.

4. Locate the CommandButton control in the Toolbox, then drag and drop it onto your form.

Figure 7-8   Here's your new UserForm, ready for you to add controls to it.

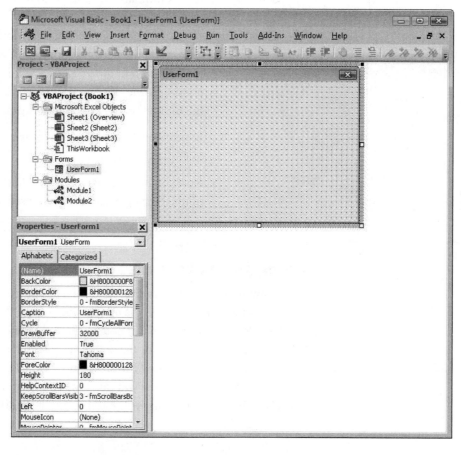

113

5. When you drop a control, it will be automatically selected (it has a gray frame around it with several drag handles you can use to resize it).

6. Drag these handles until you have a roughly square button (see Figure 7-9 for reference).

7. Repeat steps 4 through 6 to add a second button.

8. Now click the left button to select it. Then locate its Caption property in the Properties window. Notice that by default it is captioned CommandButton1, CommandButton2, or whatever number represents the order in which you added it to the form. In any case, you want the left button to be captioned *OK*. So double-click the current caption (such as CommandButton1) in the right column in the Properties window. This selects the existing name. Type in **OK** and press ENTER. Notice that the caption on the button itself immediately changes.

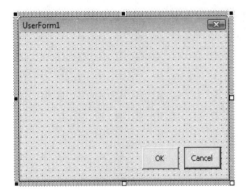

9. Repeat step 8 to change the right button's caption to Cancel.

    Now you have the set of OK and Cancel buttons typical of most dialog boxes, as you can see in Figure 7-9.

10. Now add a ListBox control to this form.

Figure 7-9   You now have the familiar OK and Cancel buttons on your UserForm.

Adding Items to a List Box

Now that you have the visible surface of your form, you need to write some code that fills the ListBox with the options you want to display to the user. To get to the code window, you can just double-click anywhere on the UserForm. But for this example, double-click the button you've captioned Cancel.

Now the code window opens, with some subs already created for you. The Editor has provided places where you can write code that responds when the user clicks either of the buttons, or the UserForm itself. (These subs that react

MEMO

If you want to quickly switch between code view and design view, click the View Code or View Object icons in the title bar of the Project Explorer, as shown in Figure 7-10.

to user clicks are called *event handlers*—a click is an event that happens, and you need to handle it with some code.)

You want to simply close this dialog box and end the execution of this little program if the user clicks the Cancel button. So add this simple code to whichever CommandButton you have captioned *Cancel*:

```
Private Sub CommandButton1_Click()
End
End Sub
```

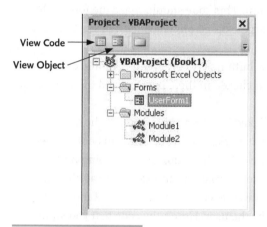

View Code
View Object

Figure 7-10   Click these icons to switch between code view and design view.

Now test this. Press F5. The UserForm is displayed. Click the Cancel button. The UserForm now disappears. Exactly what you wanted.

Now you need to add the options to the ListBox. To do this, you use the AddItem command. Back in the VB Editor, notice at the top of the code window there are two drop-down lists. Open the left one and select UserForm. The right-hand list contains all the events you can handle for the UserForm itself. In this right-hand list, click the Activate event. The Editor inserts the correct sub to handle this event.

Activation occurs when the UserForm is first created—even before the user actually sees it displayed. So this is a good place to put housekeeping code, anything that needs to be done to the form before the user interacts with it.

You want to display three font size options to the user: Small, Medium, and Large. You're designing this form, so you can name these options whatever you wish: tiny, eensie, whatever. Here's the code you should now type into the Activate event:

```
Private Sub UserForm_Activate()
ListBox1.AddItem ("Small")
ListBox1.AddItem ("Medium")
ListBox1.AddItem ("Large")
End Sub
```

115

Test this by pressing F5 and noticing how these options are displayed to the user. Click the Cancel button to close the UserForm. You might want to resize the ListBox at this point, so it fits comfortably around the displayed options—not too much blank space, but also not covering up any options. Make the box too small and the Editor will automatically add scroll bars.

Responding to the User's Selection

Our final job is to write code that reacts when the user selects an option in the ListBox and clicks the OK button. This code should make the font of the current cell small, medium, or large—based on which item in the ListBox the user chooses.

This code should go in the OK button's Click event. It should check to see which, if any, option has been clicked in the ListBox and then make the appropriate change in font size.

To figure out which item is clicked in a ListBox, you use the box's ListItem property. Here's how it works: a value of −1 means nothing was selected (so we'll just respond by closing the dialog box and doing nothing). A value of 0 means that the first item (small in this example) was clicked. A value of 1 means the second item was selected, and a value of 2 means the third item, Large, was chosen by the user. Here's the code that you should type into the OK button's Click event:

```
Private Sub CommandButton2_Click()

If ListBox1.ListIndex = 0 Then Selection.Font.Size = 8
If ListBox1.ListIndex = 1 Then Selection.Font.Size = 12
If ListBox1.ListIndex = 2 Then Selection.Font.Size = 18

End
End Sub
```

There's no need to test for the −1 (no selection) because this code only changes font size if the ListIndex is 0, 1, or 2. If the ListIndex is −1, nothing happens at all, which is the result we want.

MEMO

You might wonder why 0 represents the first item in a `ListBox`, 1 represents the second item, and so on. It's due to a mistake made decades ago when programming was just getting started. Some long-forgotten committee decided: Why waste the 0? Let's use zero as the starting value for lists! Not so good an idea, but it's too late now to fix this oddity in computer programming.

Go ahead and press F5 to see the effect of your efforts. You can of course modify this form to suit your own needs—add as many items to the list as you wish.

There is, of course, much more you can do with UserForms. You can add controls from the Toolbox to display pictures, add labels or text boxes, create sets of buttons or check boxes the user can click, and various other types of interfaces.

Link   You can find lots of sample code online. A good place to start is to choose Help | MSDN on the Web. This takes you to the gateway of a rich collection of programming examples. Or you can always use Google to search for specific code examples, such as *Excel ListBox*.

117

Using Macros to Format Cells

As you know, there are myriad formatting options available to you on the Excel ribbons. But sometimes the format selection isn't exactly what you're looking for, or sometimes there are so many formatting changes that need to be applied that the steps to reaching the desired appearance of your worksheet seem endless. You can customize the formatting tools so they meet your needs with the help of macros, and you can also automate a comprehensive formatting overhaul in macros that can be recalled into service quickly.

Using Macros to Change Existing Formats

Excel provides a selection of date formats that, on first glance, seem to cover every possible presentation of the date. But for some, the selection isn't comprehensive enough. You can post a date using your own unique style by assigning the date command and the desired style to a macro.

Looking at the U.S. date format options (right-click on a cell and choose Format Cells, then click the Date category), I see there is no option for 03/14/2001—the date, using slashes, and forcing the month to a two-digit number.

Typically when you create a customized format, the new format resides within the workbook where it was created. We can create a customized date format and make that format available to other workbooks by saving the process in a macro.

We can record this process of date customization, so let's first clear our worksheet of the formatting box. We don't want the macro recorder to record cursor movement, so place the cellpointer in any cell where you would like to see a date appear before you begin recording.

To record the new date format macro, follow these steps:

1. On the Developer ribbon, click Record Macro.

2. Enter **MyDateFormat** as the macro name.

3. Assign this macro to CTRL+SHIFT+D if you plan to use it frequently.

4. Store the macro in the Personal Macro Workbook so it will be available to all of your workbooks.

5. Enter a description, **Date format 03/14/2001** as a reminder (see Figure 8-1).

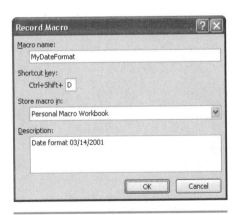

Figure 8-1   Recording our customized date style

Design your custom date format here.

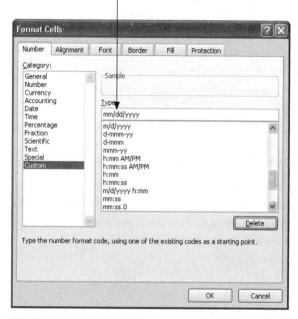

Figure 8-2 Customizing a format

6. Click OK.

7. Right-click on your active cell and choose Format Cells.

8. Choose the Custom category.

9. Scroll to find the date options, and click once on m/d/yyyy, the format closest to what we want to use.

10. In the Type field (see Figure 8-2), customize your date format to show: mm/dd/yyyy.

11. Click OK.

12. Turn off the macro recorder by clicking the Stop Recording option.

Test your macro by entering a date in the cell you just formatted. I entered 1/3/08 and my new format presented the date as 01/03/2008—just what I wanted to see! Now test your macro further by closing the workbook, opening a new workbook, and entering a date in a cell. Then press CTRL+SHIFT+D while your cellpointer is on that cell to assign the desired date format to the cell.

If you examine the code in the VB Editor, you'll see that all of those steps above resulted in one very simple line of VBA code, shown in Figure 8-3.

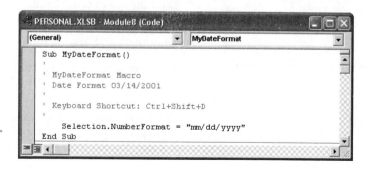

Figure 8-3 Customized MyDateFormat macro

Changing the Appearance of a Worksheet

You can create simple macros to format the different areas of your worksheet. Then, rather than hunting around the ribbons or trying to remember keyboard shortcuts or context menu commands, you can highlight an area of your worksheet, bring up your macro list, and quickly apply the type of formatting you like to use.

A Macro to Format Column Headings

This macro applies your favorite column heading style: bold, centered, and 12-point Arial font. Because the formatting features are readily available on the screen in the ribbons, you can record this macro. Select some cells to which the formatting will apply, or with just a single cell selected, follow these steps:

1. Start the macro recorder, and assign a name to the macro. I don't typically assign keyboard shortcuts to macros unless I use them quite frequently. Since I'm going to create several different formatting macros, I'm just going to assign names and not keyboard shortcuts, so that I won't confuse which shortcut goes with which macro. (Figure 8-4 shows that I am naming the macro ColumnHeadings.) Then click OK to start the recorder.

2. With the cell or cells already selected, click the Home ribbon and apply your formatting choices: Bold, Center alignment, and Arial 12 font.

3. Click the Stop Recording button at the bottom of your worksheet.

Taking a look at the VBA code that came out of that macro, in Figure 8-5, you can see first that the macro begins by applying the Bold feature to the selected

Entering a description will help you recall which formatting features this macro applies.

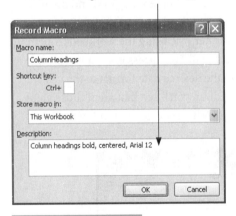

Figure 8-4   Creating a formatting macro

```
Book1 - Module1 (Code)

(General)                              ColumnHeadings

Sub ColumnHeadings()
'
' ColumnHeadings Macro
' Column headings bold, centered, Arial 12
'


    Selection.Font.Bold = True
    With Selection
        .HorizontalAlignment = xlCenter
        .VerticalAlignment = xlBottom
        .WrapText = False
        .Orientation = 0
        .AddIndent = False
        .IndentLevel = 0
        .ShrinkToFit = False
        .ReadingOrder = xlContext
        .MergeCells = False
    End With
    With Selection.Font
        .Name = "Arial"
        .Size = 12
        .Strikethrough = False
        .Superscript = False
        .Subscript = False
        .OutlineFont = False
        .Shadow = False
        .Underline = xlUnderlineStyleNone
        .ThemeColor = xlThemeColorLight1
        .TintAndShade = 0
        .ThemeFont = xlThemeFontNone
    End With
End Sub
```

Figure 8-5   Examining
recorded macro code

cells. Next there is a series of With Selection statements, applying the other choices we made to the selected cells. You can also see that there is a lot of wasted code.

You can choose to leave all of the code intact, but I recommend cleaning up the macro so that only the necessary code lines are in use. This is so that, months or even years from now, when you look back at this macro, you won't have to pore over the lines of code trying to remember what was to be accomplished. Also, if someone else examines this macro, the necessary code will be obvious and the extra lines of code will be gone. The macro will be much easier to understand.

Upon examination, I see that the first With Selection block produces a center alignment. The command for center alignment appears in the first line of code beneath the With Selection command—all the other statements in the section are not required for centering and can be removed, leaving us with the following statement.

```
With Selection
     .HorizontalAlignment = xlCenter
End With
```

The second `With Selection` segment of this macro's VBA code applies the new font selection, Arial. The rest of that code segment is unnecessary—but wait! Take a look at the second line of the code in this selection:

```
With Selection.Font
        .Name = "Arial"
        .Size = 11
End With
```

When I recorded myself imposing the Arial font upon my selected cells, the Arial font command was placed in the macro, and the default font size of 11 was also applied, along with other defaults (such as no strikethrough, no superscript, and so on). In the next `With Selection` segment of my code, the change in font size to 12 is ordered, but there's no reason why we can't consolidate a bit more and incorporate the revised font size in the same area of code as the font selection. Thus we show the two necessary lines of code, after the rest of the lines of code in the section have been removed:

```
With Selection.Font
        .Name = "Arial"
        .Size = 12
End With
```

By making this change in the code, we can now remove the entire last `With Selection` area of the VBA code. So our final macro looks like this:

```
Sub HeadingFormat()
' HeadingFormat Macro
' Bold, Centered, 12 point Arial
    Selection.Font.Bold = True
    With Selection
        .HorizontalAlignment = xlCenter
    End With
    With Selection.Font
        .Name = "Arial"
        .Size = 12
    End With
End Sub
```

A Macro to Format Number Appearance

Frequently I'll create a worksheet full of numbers, and discover that the default number format applied by Excel is not the format I want. I don't use the same format every single time, but there are a few standard formats that I use frequently enough that I'd like to be able to grab them in a hurry, with the fewest number of clicks. My favorite number formatting style is the Comma style, with no decimal places, and I prefer to have negative numbers displayed in red with parentheses.

Again, I'm going to select cells (or even just one cell) before turning on the macro recorder—this process keeps the recorder from trying to record my cell movements or mouse selection. That way I can easily apply the format to any cells simply by selecting the cells, and then running the macro.

Here are the steps for creating a macro that will apply my favorite style of number formatting.

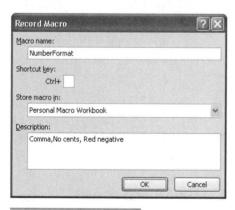

Figure 8-6   Recording the NumberFormat macro

1. Turn on the macro recorder. Name this macro, save it to the Personal Macro Workbook, and provide a brief description, similar to the example in Figure 8-6. Then click OK to begin recording.

2. Apply the number formats you like to the selected cell(s). You can click on the Home ribbon to find some of the number format tools, or you can right-click on the selected cell(s), choose Format Cells, and then Number, and then make your formatting selections (see Figure 8-7). Click OK to apply your choices.

3. If there are font formats you want to apply to your numbers, such as a font selection, an alignment, or an underline feature, you can make those selections at this time as well.

4. When all formatting selections have been made, turn off the macro recorder.

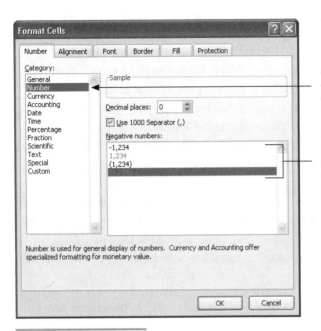

Click the Number tab to display formatting options.

Select options for decimal places, comma usage, and negative number presentation.

Figure 8-7   Choosing a number format

Test your macro by entering some numbers in a new area of your workbook, and then choosing your NumberFormat macro from the Macros list.

Once again, it makes sense to examine your macro code for unnecessary lines of code. If you only applied a number format, the code is simple and does not need scouring. If you applied font selections as well, there may be lines of code that can be removed to streamline the code and make it more understandable. Here is the code for my NumberFormat macro:

```
Sub NumberFormat()
' NumberFormat Macro
' Comma,No cents, No zeros
    Selection.NumberFormat = "#,##0_);[Red](#,##0)"
End Sub
```

Change the Appearance of a Worksheet

Sometimes you want to change not just the appearance of numbers or headings, but the appearance of the worksheet as a whole. Perhaps you want to display the worksheet without gridlines, or maybe you want to adjust the width of columns. You might prefer a specific font style and size. We can create a macro that applies these specifications to a worksheet.

Depending on the types of changes you want to apply, you can preselect either the entire worksheet (by clicking in the box to the left of the Column A letter), or you can select some columns or some rows. In preparation for recording this macro, think about what will be affected. If you're going to adjust column width, you'll need to select some columns. Likewise, you'll need to select some rows if you want to adjust row height.

For this example of a macro to change the appearance of a spreadsheet, I'm going to select the entire worksheet after I begin recording. My macro, which I'll call MyWorksheetSetup, will remove gridlines, adjust column width to nine characters, and set Arial as the font on the entire worksheet.

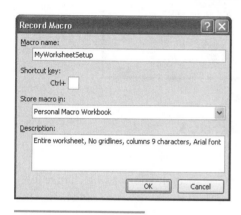

Figure 8-8   Formatting a worksheet

1. Turn on the macro recorder. Name the macro, store it in the Personal Macro Workbook, and provide a brief description, similar to Figure 8-8.

2. Click the Select All button in the upper-left corner of the worksheet.

3. Click the Page Layout ribbon, and then uncheck the View box beneath the Gridlines heading.

4. Slide one of the column bars between column letter headings so that the new column width for selected columns is nine characters.

5. Change the font on the Home ribbon to Arial.

6. Turn off the macro recorder.

127

Test the macro by opening a new workbook and running the macro. Examining the VBA code, I can see that the only change I might want to make is to remove the extraneous code in the `With Selection.Font` area, where the only code I need is this:

```
With Selection.Font
    .Name = "Arial"
End With
```

The completed macro appears in Figure 8-9.

Figure 8-9   Macro code for changing worksheet formatting

Changing a Worksheet Color Scheme

Here's a quick little macro that you can use to apply a formatting change to the background color of your worksheet. With this macro, you can change the appearance of the rows on your worksheet so that every other row is green—just like the old computer printouts of the '70s and '80s.

This macro uses some features that are discussed in greater depth elsewhere in this book, but since the macro deals primarily with formatting, it seems appropriate to include it here. There is a For/Next loop in this macro—you'll learn how to create your own For/Next loops in Chapter 11. You'll also create a variable in this macro. This gives you a head start on the next chapter, Chapter 9, which is all about variables.

To use this macro, you select an area of your worksheet. Within this macro, which I've called AlternateColor, a variable is created to indicate the number of rows you selected. Then the macro counts by 2, and applies a color shading to the alternating rows. This is not a macro you can record, so you have to create this macro in the VB Editor.

```
Sub AlternateColor
Dim i as Long
For i = 1 to Selection.Rows.Count Step 2
     Selection.Rows(i).Interior.ColorIndex = 35
Next
End Sub
```

The line "`Dim i as Long`" uses the VBA `Dim` or `Dimension` statement to assign a variable, in this case named "i". The phrase '`Dim variable as Long`' defines the variable as an integer.

The `For/Next` loop, which is discussed in more detail in Chapter 11, simply states that you take the rows in the selection area, starting with 1, and continuing to the end of the selection, you step by 2, meaning you go to every other line, and you apply an interior color, or a shading. In this case, I have selected number 35 from the Excel Color Index (see the following Link). To use a different color for your shading, simply change the 35 to another number on the color index.

Using and Combining Formatting Macros

Now that we've completed several macros that provide formatting changes for our worksheets, it's time to consider ways in which these macros can be used.

When building a worksheet, just as you would select an area and apply formatting changes to that area, you can select an area and click the Macro list to display formatting macros that are available. Each macro we've created combines several formatting tools, and you can apply those tools with one macro choice instead of having to perform each task separately.

When you display the macro list, all of the macros in the Personal Macro Workbook appear, along with any macros saved in your current workbook, and any macros that are

Link You can view the Excel color palette with it's corresponding numbers at http://www.mvps.org/dmcritchie/excel/colors.htm.

saved in other workbooks currently open. Choose one of your formatting macros, click the Run button, and all the formatting tasks you loaded into the chosen macro are applied to the area of the worksheet you selected. Or, if you created a macro like the MyWorksheetSetup macro that was designed to format an entire worksheet, you don't need to select any cells before running the macro.

Combining Macros

You can take pieces of the macros you created and make new mega-macros, combining the pieces that you find useful. For example, previously we created the MyWorksheetSetup macro that formatted the appearance of the entire worksheet. We also created the NumberFormat macro, changing the formatting for number cells in the selected area.

The MyWorksheetSetup macro performs the task of selecting all the cells in the worksheet. Why not take the customized number format and apply that to all of the cells as well? We can grab the code from the NumberFormat macro, place that code in the MyWorksheetSetup macro, and now the entire worksheet will also have customized number formatting, all done by running one single macro. Here's how it works:

1. Open the VB Editor.

2. Find the NumberFormat macro.

3. Copy the line of code that applies your customized number format to the selection:

   ```
   Selection.NumberFormat = "#,##0_);[Red](#,##0)"
   ```

4. Find the code for the MyWorksheetSetup macro.

5. Insert the line of code that you copied from the NumberFormat macro. The code can be placed anywhere after the `Cells.Select` line and before the `With/End With` segment.

6. Save your changes (CTRL+S).

130

MEMO

Be sure to copy and not cut the code from the number formatting macro. We still want to keep that macro intact, so don't remove any code line; just copy the code to the clipboard.

Here's the revised MyWorksheetSetup macro:

```
Sub MyWorksheetSetup()
' MyWorksheetSetup Macro
' Entire worksheet, No gridlines, columns 9 characters, Arial font
    Cells.Select
    ActiveWindow.DisplayGridlines = False
    Selection.ColumnWidth = 9
    Selection.NumberFormat = "#,##0_);[Red](#,##0)"
    With Selection.Font
        .Name = "Arial"
    End With
End Sub
```

Test this macro on a new workbook and you should find that, in addition to the other formatting changes we placed in the MyWorksheetSetup macro, now the number formatting has been applied as well.

Using VBA Commands to Select Worksheet Areas

So far we've either selected an area of the worksheet before recording a macro, so that when we run the macro, we will select the applicable cells, and then run the macro, or we have selected the entire worksheet within the macro and then applied macro formatting commands to the entire worksheet.

You can also arrange for an area to be selected within the macro. Here are some common macro commands that select specific areas on your worksheet:

- **ActiveCell.CurrentRegion.Select**   Selects the specified range beginning with the current cell.

- **Cells(Rownumber,Columnnumber)**   Selects a particular cell location.

- **Range("Rangename")**   Selects a named range (the range name appears in quotes).

- **`Range(Cells(startcell),Cells(endcell))`** Selects a range by giving the beginning and ending coordinates. Cell references are given in numerical terms—cell B5 is shown as Cells(2.5).

- **`Selection.EntireColumn`** Selects the current column.

- **`Selection.EntireRow`** Selects the current row.

Try creating a macro by entering commands in the VB Editor that include a selection command. Here's an example of a macro that will change the appearance of the specified region beginning with the current cell, so that the cells in the region become bold and the columns are set to the best fit.

```
Sub BoldFormat()
ActiveCell.CurrentRegion.Select
    Selection.Font.Bold = True
    Selection.EntireColumn.AutoFit
ActiveCell.Select
End Sub
```

To test this macro, open a workbook and enter some information in adjacent cells. The `CurrentRegion` command looks for a specified region of cells, so in this case, the adjacent cells that are filled will receive the benefit of this macro formatting. Figure 8-10 shows a range of cells before applying the BoldFormat macro, and Figure 8-11 shows the same range after applying the BoldFormat macro.

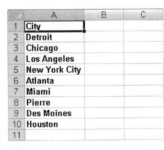

Figure 8-10 Before the Bold-Format macro is applied

Figure 8-11 After the BoldFormat macro is applied

Using Variables in Macros

Variables are a major feature of any kind of programming, macros included. In fact, variables are common in many ordinary situations in life. For example, your town's weather, your monthly VISA debt, and your appetite are all variables. In its most general sense, a variable is simply something that changes. This chapter explores variables and related issues such as *expressions, operators,* and *arrays.*

Why Use Variables?

You create variables in a macro for the same reason that you might have a manila envelope in your desk with the word *VISA* written on it. Each month you put your most recent VISA statement inside. Each time you get a new bill, you replace last month's bill with the latest bill. So the general concept of a variable is: a labeled container that holds a piece of information.

Now, the datum in a variable doesn't have to change when a program executes. (I say *datum* because each variable contains only a single value—a number or a text string.) For example, you might not use your VISA card for several months, so the debt value remains the same. Or you might live in San Diego, and the weather is identical for months. But a variable has the ability to change, and this gives it power in a program.

A variable's value (its datum) can change based on user input or based on actions that take place within the macro as it runs. For example, if you write a macro that manages your personal finances, you might use an input box to allow the user to enter this month's VISA debt. So that variable changes based on user input. But a variable containing your current net worth will change based on calculations the macro carries out, such as subtracting food expenses, adding interest income, and so on.

In a macro you can use the variable's name in place of its datum (the number or text string it contains). If you put your current VISA bill each month in your envelope, you can always look in this envelope labeled VISA to find out how much you owe at the current time. Similarly, once a variable is created in a running macro, a location in the computer's memory contains that variable's name along with its "contents," the information that this variable "holds" until, or if, the contents are changed by the running program.

You've already used variables various times in the code examples in this book. Macros would be difficult to write without using variables. Let's use an example from Chapter 7:

```
Sub GetInitials()
    x = InputBox("Please enter your initials", "Enter Initials")
```

```
        Range("A1").Select
        ActiveCell.FormulaR1C1 = x
End Sub
```

In this macro, you ask the user to type in his or her initials, and then display the initials in a cell. The variable in this macro is X. Each person who runs this macro is likely to type in different initials, so the value in X varies. While the macro executes, this datum is retained. But when the macro stops executing, the datum is lost and must be retyped the next time the macro executes. However, before this macro finishes executing, it uses X a second time to enter the datum in a cell.

Naming Variables

In the previous example, I used the simple name X for my variable. But you can use any names you wish for your variables, as long as you follow a few simple rules. A variable name must

- Start with a letter, so 12Months is not permitted, but Months12 is.

- Not include any of the words already used by VBA itself, such as If, Sub, or End.

- Not be longer than 255 characters.

- Not include special characters such as punctuation marks, brackets, the percent symbol (or any other of those symbols above the numbers in the top row of keys). So My% is not permitted, although MyPercent is.

Fortunately, it doesn't matter how you capitalize. MyPercent is seen as the same variable as mypercent or MYPERCENT. So you can mix and match capitalization as you wish and VBA will still treat these case variations as the same, single variable. Of course if you *spell* the name wrong, you can cause errors. To VBA, MyPercent and MyyPercent are two different variables. (This particular error can be avoided by explicitly declaring all your variables. See the briefing later in this chapter.)

135

MEMO

These same naming restrictions also apply to other things you name in VBA, such as modules, subs, and so on. VBA will tell you if you use an improper name by displaying a Syntax Error message (when naming variables), or if you try to name a module incorrectly, you'll see a *Not a Legal Object Name* error message.

Creating a Variable

You can create a variable by simply using it. You can use it with an object such as an input box as in the previous code example from Chapter 7. Or another common way to use (and thus create) a variable is to just assign some value to the variable, like this:

```
Donkeys = 15
```

This act simultaneously creates the variable's name and assigns a value to it. In this example, you have provided a label (a variable name)—*Donkeys*—and said that there are 15 donkeys. The user never sees this label, *Donkeys*.

DECLARATIONS AND TYPES

Formal variable declaration: some people swear by it, others swear at it. What's the truth? Actually, declaring variables is considered essential for large programs, but with macros, not so much.

Macros are generally small and self-sufficient, so you can usually just safely ignore a couple of features involving variables: declaring them and specifying the variable's type. Yes, there are several types of variables: string (text), integer (no decimal point), floating point (has a decimal point and therefore can express fractional numbers), and so on.

But in more advanced, complex programming it's considered a good idea to formally, explicitly declare each variable. Here's how it's done:

```
Sub GetInitials()
    Dim x As String
    x = InputBox("Please enter your
initials", "Enter Initials")

    Range("A1").Select
    ActiveCell.FormulaR1C1 = x
End Sub
```

The Dim command declares a variable. Dim tells VBA that we are now creating a new variable. In the example above, we declare that this new variable's name is X and that it is a string variable type.

Recall that if you don't include this Dim line of code in your macro, VBA will still automatically create this variable X for you (this is called *implicit declaration*). So what's the value of explicit declaration?

Formally declaring a variable can help avoid a couple of bugs (mistyping a variable's name elsewhere in the code, or causing VBA to incorrectly interpret a variable's type and thus produce a wrong answer).

However, some say that for beginners writing macros, it's overkill to worry about explicit declaration. But go ahead and declare all your variables if you wish.

One more issue: if you leave out explicit declarations, which variable type does VBA use when implicitly creating variables? It uses a special, all-purpose type called the *variant*—allowing VBA to automatically manage the whole issue of variable typing for you.

You use it for programming purposes, and you can give it a name that means something to you.

Most programmers give variables names that help them to understand the meaning or purpose of the variable. A variable named X is less useful than one named *Donkeys*. Descriptive variable names can make it easier to read your code, and easier to test or modify your macro. However, when the purpose of a variable is obvious (such as an input box that requests the user's initials), go ahead and use brief labels like X or S or whatever.

Combining Variables into Expressions

Variables can interact with each other. Here's an example showing how they can interact mathematically, adding one variable to another to produce a third variable:

```
Donkeys = 15
Monkeys = 3
TotalAnimals = Donkeys + Monkeys
```

As the third line illustrates, you can use *variables' names* as if they were the same as the contents of the variables. If you say Monkeys = 3, then you have assigned the value 3 to the word *Monkeys*. You can thereafter use *Monkeys* just as you would use the number 3:

```
TotalAnimals = Donkeys + Monkeys
```

The preceding line is the same as the following:

```
TotalAnimals = Donkeys + 3
```

The number itself (3 in this example) is called a *literal* because it's literally three, literally a value. String literals are in quotes: "Thomas" is a string literal. When you combine variables with variables (such as Donkeys + Monkeys) or combine variables with literals (such as Donkeys + 3), you have created an *expression*.

What exactly is an *expression*? If someone tells you she has *a coupon for $1 off a $15 Amy Winehouse CD*, you immediately think *$14*. In the same way, VB reduces the several items linked into an expression into its simplest form. This action, reducing something into a simpler form, is called evaluation.

In plain English: If you type 15 – 1 into one of your programs, Visual Basic reduces that group of symbols, that *expression*, to a single number: 14. Visual Basic simply evaluates what you've said and uses it in the program as the essence of what you are trying to say.

An expression is made up of two or more variables (or literals) connected *by one or more* operators. We'll get to *operators* shortly. The plus sign in 2 + 2 is an operator. Altogether there are 23 operators you can use in your macro programming.

Certain operators, such as > (greater than), cause expressions to be evaluated as either true or false (zero represents false, any other number represents true). Let's see how this works:

```
BobsAge = 33
BettysAge = 27
If BobsAge > BettysAge Then MsgBox "He's Older"
```

`BobsAge > BettysAge` is an expression. This expression claims that *BobsAge* is greater than *BettysAge*. The greater than (>) symbol is one of several *comparison operators*. Visual Basic looks at the variables *BobsAge* and *BettysAge* and at the relational operator that combines them into the expression. VB then determines whether or not the expression is actually true. The `If...Then` structure bases its actions on the truth or falsity of the expression.

In this case, the message box is displayed because the expression is true. However, if you change BettysAge to 33 or anything higher, then the message box will not be displayed. The expression will evaluate to `False`.

Understanding Operators

The > (greater than) operator is only one of many operators. The following section describes all the other operators.

MEMO

Special Note on Mod: The Modulo (Mod) operator gives you any remainder after a division—but not the results of the division itself. This operation is useful when you want to know if some number divides evenly into another number. That way, you could write a macro that takes actions at intervals. For example, if you wanted to print the page number in bold on every fifth page, you could enter the following:

```
If PageNumber Mod
5 = 0 Then
FontBold =
True
Else
FontBold
= 0
End If
```

15 Mod 5 results in 0. 16 Mod 5 results in 1. 17 Mod 5 results in 2. But 20 Mod 5 results in 0 again.

Comparison Operators

Comparison operators always return simply a true or false answer.

<	Less than
<=	Less than or equal to
>	Greater than
>=	Greater than or equal to
<>	Not equal
=	Equal
Is	Do two object variables refer to the same object?
Like	Pattern matching

Arithmetic Operators

∧	Exponentiation (the number multiplied by itself: $5 \wedge 2$ is 25 and $5 \wedge 3$ is 125)
−	Negation (negative numbers, such as −25)
*	Multiplication
/	Division
\	Integer division (This kind of division provides no remainder, no fraction, no *floating-point* decimal point: 8 \ 6 results in 1. Integer division is easier, and the computer performs it faster than regular division.)
Mod	Modulo arithmetic (See the Memo on the left.)
+	Addition
−	Subtraction
&	String concatenation

Logical Operators

Not	Logical negation
And	And
Or	Inclusive Or
XOR	(Either but not Both)
Eqv	(Equivalent)
Imp	(Implication—first item False or second item True)

In practice, you'll likely need to use only And, Not, and Or from among the logical operators. These operators mostly work pretty much the way they do in English. Here's an example showing how to use Or:

```
If 5 + 2 = 4 Or 6 + 6 = 12 Then MsgBox "One of them is true."
```

One of these expressions *is* in fact true. Six and six equals 12. So the message will be displayed. Only one OR the other expression needs to be true in this case.

However, if you use the AND operator instead, then both expressions must be true for the message to be displayed:

```
If 5 + 2 = 4 And 6 + 6 = 12 Then MsgBox "Both of them are true."
```

This evaluates to False, so no message is displayed.

The String Operator

The & operator adds (concatenates) pieces of text together:

```
N = "Lois"
N1 = "Lane"
J = N & " " & N1
MsgBox J
```

Results in: Lois Lane

Operator Precedence

One last issue involving expressions needs to be explored: precedence.

When you use more than one operator in an expression, which operator should be evaluated first? Which operator takes precedence over the other?

Understanding What Gets Evaluated First

Here's an example that uses the multiplication operator and the addition operator:

```
Msgbox 3 * 10 + 5
```

Does this expression mean first multiply 3 times 10, getting 30? And then add 5 to the result? Should VBA display 35 in the message box?

Or does it mean add 10 to 5, getting 15, then multiply the result by 3? *This* would result in 45. As you can see, there's ambiguity here. This expression can be evaluated two different ways, resulting in two different answers. We can't have that.

To make sure that you get the results you intend when using more than one operator, use parentheses to enclose the items you want evaluated first. If you intended to say 3 * 10 and then add 5, write it like this in your macro:

```
MsgBox (3 * 10) + 5
```

By enclosing that 3 * 10 in parentheses, you tell VBA that you want the enclosed items to be considered a single value and to be evaluated before anything else happens.

But if you intended to say first add 10 + 5, and then multiply the result by 3, write it like this:

```
MsgBox 3 * (10 + 5)
```

In complicated expressions, you can even *nest* parentheses to make clear which items are to be calculated in which order. Here I've used two sets of parentheses:

```
MsgBox 3 * ((9 + 1) + 5)
```

VBA, however, does have a built-in order of precedence. Therefore, if you wish, you can leave out the parentheses. If you work with numbers a great deal, you might prefer to memorize the following list, which illustrates the order of precedence, with exponentiation being carried out first, negation next, and so on.

Although most people just use parentheses and can forget about this whole problem, here's the order in which VBA will evaluate an expression, from first evaluated to last:

Arithmetic Operators in Order of Precedence

∧	Exponents (6 ∧ 2 is 36. The number is multiplied by itself *X* number of times.)
–	Negation (negative numbers like –33)
* /	Multiplication and division
\	Integer division
Mod	Modulo arithmetic (any remainder after division)
+ –	Addition and subtraction
The relational operators	
The logical operators	

Arrays: Cluster Variables

Arrays are variables that have been clustered together. Inside an array structure, the variables share the same text name, but each one has its own unique index number. Since numbers can be manipulated mathematically (and text names cannot), putting a group of variables into an array allows you to easily and efficiently work with them as a group. You can manipulate the elements (the individual items) in the array by using loops such as For . . . Next described in Chapter 11.

Arrays are used in computer programming for the same reason ZIP codes are used by the U.S. Postal Service. Picture hundreds of postal boxes with only text labels. Imagine the nightmare of sorting thousands of letters each day into boxes that are not in some way indexed and numerically ordered.

Numbers vs. Names

Arrays can be extremely useful, particularly in longer or more complex programs. For example, if you want to manage data about a group of people coming to dinner this weekend, you can create an array of their names, like this:

```
Dim Guest (1 To 5) As String
```

This creates five "empty boxes" in the computer's memory, and each box can hold a single piece of text. However, instead of five unique individual labels for the five variables, the variables share the name Guest, and each box is identified by a unique index number from 1 to 5.

To fill this array with the names of the guests, you can assign the names just as you would assign them to normal variables, but use the array name plus the index number, like this:

```
Guest(1) = "Lois"
Guest(2) = "Sandy Pourettez from work"
Guest(3) = "Rick"
Guest(4) = "Jim"
Guest(5) = "Mom"
```

You can tell an array from a regular variable because arrays always have parentheses following the array name. The index number goes between these parentheses.

Now that you have the array filled, you can manipulate it in ways that are much more efficient than using ordinary variables. For example, searching. What if we wanted to know if a particular name existed in the array? You can use a For...Next loop to examine the array:

```
For I = 1 To 5
    If Guest(I) = "Rick" Then Print "Rick has been invited."
Next I
```

143

The key to the utility of arrays is that you can search them, sort them, delete them, or add to them by *using their index numbers* to identify each item. Index numbers are much easier to access and manipulate than individual variable names.

Suppose you need to figure your average electric bill for the year. You could go the cumbersome route, using an individual variable name for each month, like this:

```
JanElect = 90
FebElect = 122
MarElect = 125
AprElect = 78
MayElect = 144
JneElect = 89
JulyElect = 90
AugElect = 140
SeptElect = 167
OctElect = 123
NovElect = 133
DecElect = 125
YearElectBill = JanElect+FebElect+MarElect+AprElect+MayElect+
JneElect+JulyElect+AugElect+SeptElect+OctElect+NovElect+DecElect
```

Or you could just use an array to simplify the process:

```
Dim MonthElectBill(1 To 12)
MonthElectBill(1)  = 90
MonthElectBill(2)  = 122
MonthElectBill(3)  = 125
MonthElectBill(4)  = 78
MonthElectBill(5)  = 144
MonthElectBill(6)  = 89
MonthElectBill(7)  = 90
MonthElectBill(8)  = 140
MonthElectBill(9)  = 167
MonthElectBill(10) = 123
```

```
MonthElectBill(11) = 133
MonthElectBill(12) = 125

For I = 1 to 12
Total = Total + MonthElectBill(I)
Next I
```

By grouping all the variables under the same array name, you can manipulate the variables by individual index number. This might look like a small saving of effort, but remember that data-intensive programs can manipulate large amounts of data, or may need to reuse the same data in several different parts of the program.

So the moral is, if you're dealing with only a little bit of data (like the user's name and address), ordinary variables work fine. But if you are working with larger amounts of data—especially data that's related in some way, such as a year's worth of electric bills—arrays are a more efficient approach.

Creating an Array

The simplest way to declare an array is to use the Dim command:

```
Dim ArraysName (1 To 12)
```

MEMO

There are several kinds of arrays, but we'll stick to the simplest in this book. You can also create arrays with more than one "dimension." They are similar to a worksheet with multiple columns, or indeed a set of data covering multiple worksheets. But this type of array is generally not found in macros.

The Dim command is said to *dimension* (make space for) the new array. The computer is told how much space to set aside for the new array.

To create space for 51 text variables that share the name Employees and are uniquely identified by index numbers ranging from 1–100, type the following in a module:

```
Dim Employees(1 To 100)
```

You can visualize this array as similar to the first column in an Excel worksheet: A1:A100. Each cell can contain a single number or piece of text, and you refer to each of them by the same name (A in this case) and also by the cell's number from 1 to 100.

Array Rules

Here are a few rules to follow when working with arrays.

You should try to anticipate the number of elements you'll need in an array, but be generous and add a bit more. For example, if you have 40 employees, you might provide room for 100, just in case the company grows. So use 1 To 100 rather than 1 To 40 when declaring that array.

You can name arrays just the same way you name variables: the names are case-insensitive, but must follow the rules explained earlier in this chapter in the section titled "Naming Variables."

Unlike variables, arrays cannot be implicitly declared by simply using them. You must formally declare each array with the Dim command (or related commands).

Creating If/Then/Else Routines

You can use If/Then/Else routines to give logic to your macros. The process of the macro proceeds in different directions depending on the results of an If command. Just like the IF function in Excel, the If/Then/Else command relies on a logical statement with a true scenario and a false scenario.

We saw one If/Then/Else command in Chapter 6, where we created a macro that asked the user which print area he wanted to print (see the following box). Here's a plain-language description of how the macro works. The macro analyzes the user response by determining that, if the user enters 1, then print PrintArea1, and the macro then ends. The macro logic continues, however, with an ElseIf command that allows for the user to enter something other than a 1. If the user enters something other than 1, the macro doesn't end and instead proceeds to the next step, which determines that, if the user enters 2, then print PrintArea2, and then end the macro. Finally, if the user enters a wrong answer, that is, something other than 1 or 2, the macro contains a provision to return to the original question and give the user another chance. (Note that the user also has the right to cancel the macro operation at any time by clicking a Cancel button.)

SPECIAL PRINT MACRO FROM CHAPTER 6

```
Sub SpecialPrint()
Question:
Report = InputBox("Enter 1 to print Report 1; Enter 2 to print Report 2")
If Report = 1 Then
      GoTo Print1
ElseIf Report = 2 Then
      GoTo Print2
Else
      GoTo Question
End If
Print1:
      Application.Goto Reference:="PrintArea1"
      ExecuteExcel4Macro "PRINT(1,,,1,,,,,,,,1,,,TRUE,,FALSE)"
      End
Print2:
      Application.Goto Reference:="PrintArea2"
      ExecuteExcel4Macro "PRINT(1,,,1,,,,,,,,1,,,TRUE,,FALSE)"
      End
End sub
```

148

The success of any If/Then/Else routine comes from anticipating all the possible responses and providing commands to deal with each possible condition.

MEMO

The Else statement in the If/Then/Else routine is not a required command in this If/Then structure. You can create If/Then routines that do not include an alternate direction provided by the Else statement.

Understanding the If/Then/Else Routine

When you enter an If statement in your macro, the If precedes a logical statement. It is up to Visual Basic to determine if this statement is true or false. This statement that follows If is called a *conditional expression*. The condition of this statement can be either true or false. If it is a true statement, the macro proceeds to do what it is told to do in the Then statement.

If you only want an action to occur when the statement is true, then your macro is finished when you have an If and a Then statement.

Create a Simple If/Then Macro

For example, say you have a worksheet that contains numbers that represent annual sales figures. If the sales figure exceeds 100,000, then you want the macro to calculate a bonus by placing a figure in the cell to the right that equates to the original figure times 2 percent.

Before you jump into programming this little macro, think through the process in baby steps. Here are all the things that this macro needs to do:

- Examine the number in the current cell and determine if it is larger than 100,000.

- If the number is larger than 100,000, move the cellpointer one cell to the right.

- Enter a calculation in the new cell that multiplies the number in the original cell by 2 percent.

Some of this macro can be recorded so that you can harvest the code. You can record yourself moving the cellpointer one cell to the right, and you can record the creation of the formula. The only thing you can't record is the If/Then statement.

Recording the cellpointer movement and the formula yields this macro code:

```
ActiveCell.Offset(0, 1).Range("A1").Select
ActiveCell.FormulaR1C1 = "=RC[-1]*0.02"
ActiveCell.Offset(1, 0).Range("A1").Select
```

MEMO

Because we want to use this macro on several different cells, be sure to turn on the Relative References feature before turning on the macro recorder.

The first line of code reflects the movement of the cellpointer from the original cell to the cell to the right—Offset(0,1) shows movement of 0 rows and 1 column forward (or right).

The second line of the code provides the formula: No row movement, but one column back, times 0.02.

The third line of the code moves the cellpointer down one cell, a circumstance that naturally occurs when you press ENTER. Offset(1,0) refers to an advance of 1 row and 0 columns. If instead you want the cellpointer to move to the next cell in the column of existing numbers (in anticipation of applying this macro to the next number), then you should change the offset to (1,–1).

Now all you need in order to have this macro make the logical decision is the If statement that asks if the original cell contains a number greater than 100000.

```
If ActiveCell.Value > 100000 Then
```

The preceding line of code asks if the value of the active cell is greater than 100,000. If the answer is true, then the next line of the VBA code executes. If the answer is false, nothing happens.

Note one final thing—any time you use an If/Then statement, you must conclude the If/Then section with an End If statement.

Thus the final macro code looks like this:

```
Sub Bonus()
'
' Macro to calculate bonus
'
    If ActiveCell.Value > 100000 Then
    ActiveCell.Offset(0, 1).Range("A1").Select
    ActiveCell.FormulaR1C1 = "=RC[-1]*0.02"
    ActiveCell.Offset(1, -1).Range("A1").Select
    End If
End Sub
```

To execute this macro, place your cellpointer on a cell containing a number that you want to analyze. Click the Macros button to find your macro on the list, click on the macro, and then click Run. If the number you chose is greater than 100,000, your Then sequence is activated and the calculation appears in the cell to the right of the original number. The cellpointer returns to the cell beneath the original number (see Figure 10-1).

	A	B	C	D
1	Annual sales			
2	2000	121578	2431.56	
3	2001	105775	2115.5	
4	2002	98255		
5	2003	168540	3370.8	
6	2004	124851	2497.02	
7	2005	95123		
8	2006	99123		
9	2007	100254	2005.08	
10				
11				

Figure 10-1   The worksheet after the macro has executed

Add an Else Operation for a False Answer

So far we've created a macro that analyzes a situation, and if the situation is true, a command is executed. If the situation is not true, the macro ends. But we don't have to stop there. We can tell the macro to perform some other task if the answer to the initial question is false. In the Bonus macro that we already created, the macro does nothing if the sales figure is less than 100,000. Instead, we can make the macro continue to the Bonus column and enter a zero.

You can record yourself performing this task if you like, but if you look at the macro code that already exists, it should be a pretty simple step to add the Else clause to this macro, without even recording. We want our Else clause to have the operation move one cell to the right (we already have that code in place), and then enter zero. This code should do the trick:

```
ActiveCell.FormulaR1C1 = "0"
```

Then you also need another line of code to provide instructions for where the cellpointer should end up—just as in the Then part of the macro:

```
ActiveCell.Offset(1, -1).Range("A1").Select
```

And so the completed macro, with instructions for how to behave if the statement is true and if it is false, looks like this:

```
Sub Bonus()
' Macro to calculate bonus
    If ActiveCell.Value > 100000 Then
        ActiveCell.Offset(0, 1).Range("A1").Select
        ActiveCell.FormulaR1C1 = "=RC[-1]*0.02"
        ActiveCell.Offset(1, -1).Range("A1").Select
    Else
        ActiveCell.Offset(0, 1).Range("A1").Select
        ActiveCell.FormulaR1C1 = "0"
        ActiveCell.Offset(1, -1).Range("A1").Select
    End If
End Sub
```

Add an ElseIf Operation

So we've seen how to create a macro containing an If/Then/Else statement, and that handles the situation when there is only one right and one wrong answer. Now we'll take this a level deeper, and add a second If statement, known as an ElseIf statement, so that if the macro returns a false answer to the first If statement, there is another opportunity for a true statement to occur.

This time we'll add a level of the macro that occurs after the first If statement executes and produces a false answer. Instead of immediately assuming there is no bonus to compute and placing a zero in the Bonus cell, we'll apply a second criterion—the ability to calculate a bonus if the sales figure exceeds 75000. This time the bonus calculation will be 1 percent instead of 2 percent. So the complete bonus calculation is 2 percent if sales exceed 100,000 and 1 percent if sales are in the 75,000 to 100,000 range.

You can probably figure out this new piece of code without recording any steps. As a reminder, here's the code that calculates the first bonus:

```
If ActiveCell.Value > 100000 Then
    ActiveCell.Offset(0, 1).Range("A1").Select
    ActiveCell.FormulaR1C1 = "=RC[-1]*0.02"
    ActiveCell.Offset(1, -1).Range("A1").Select
```

Now here's all you have to do add an ElseIf layer that asks if the ActiveCell.Value exceeds 75,000, and applies a 1 percent bonus:

```
ElseIf ActiveCell.Value > 75000 Then
    ActiveCell.Offset(0, 1).Range("A1").Select
    ActiveCell.FormulaR1C1 = "=RC[-1]*0.01"
    ActiveCell.Offset(1, -1).Range("A1").Select
```

The ElseIf format works the same way as the If code—you must accompany the ElseIf statement with a Then statement. This piece of new code can be inserted in the macro. The finished product appears in Figure 10-2. The results appear in Figure 10-3.

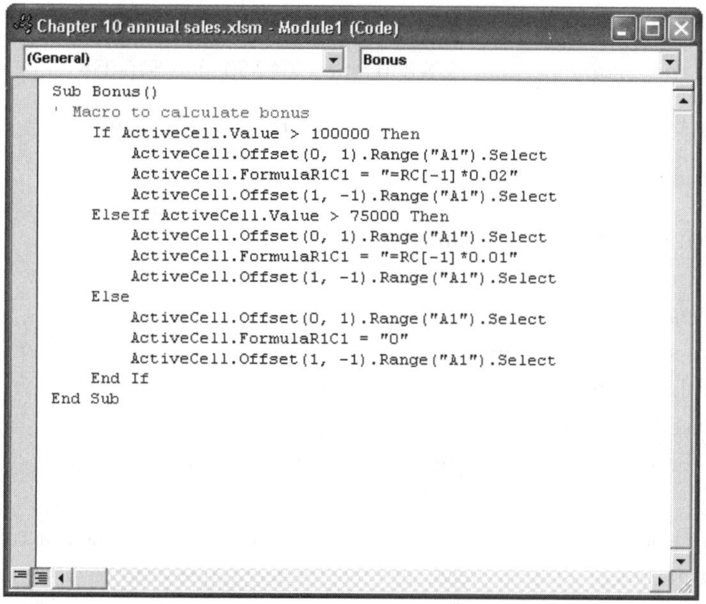

```
Chapter 10 annual sales.xlsm - Module1 (Code)

(General)                                      Bonus

Sub Bonus()
' Macro to calculate bonus
    If ActiveCell.Value > 100000 Then
        ActiveCell.Offset(0, 1).Range("A1").Select
        ActiveCell.FormulaR1C1 = "=RC[-1]*0.02"
        ActiveCell.Offset(1, -1).Range("A1").Select
    ElseIf ActiveCell.Value > 75000 Then
        ActiveCell.Offset(0, 1).Range("A1").Select
        ActiveCell.FormulaR1C1 = "=RC[-1]*0.01"
        ActiveCell.Offset(1, -1).Range("A1").Select
    Else
        ActiveCell.Offset(0, 1).Range("A1").Select
        ActiveCell.FormulaR1C1 = "0"
        ActiveCell.Offset(1, -1).Range("A1").Select
    End If
End Sub
```

	A	B	C	D
1	Annual sales			
2	2000	121578	2431.56	
3	2001	105775	2115.5	
4	2002	98255	982.55	
5	2003	168540	3370.8	
6	2004	124851	2497.02	
7	2005	95123	951.23	
8	2006	72451	0	
9	2007	100254	2005.08	
10				
11				

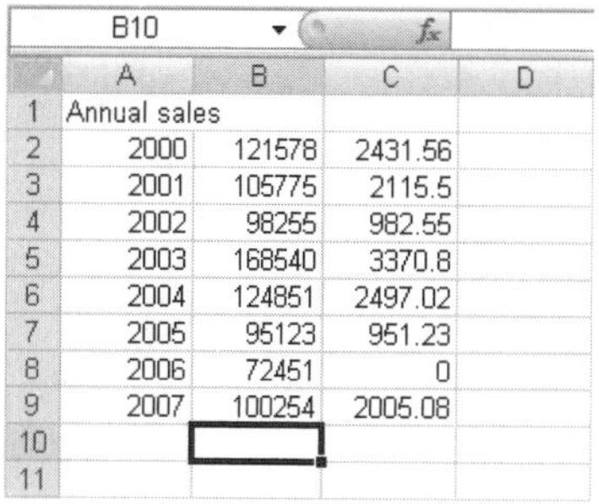

Figure 10-3   The Bonus results based on the calculations in the Bonus macro

Figure 10-2   The finished If/Then/Else macro

MEMO

In Chapter 11 you'll learn about creating For/Next loops and you'll be able to apply that skill to macros like this If/Then/Else macro so that you don't have to call the macro on each cell—the macro can run through the entire list of sales figures with one command.

Create a Multilevel If/Then/Else Macro

Back in Chapter 6, you learned how to create a macro using the Case command to offer the user a selection of several different criteria. We created one macro that calculated U.S. corporate income tax. We can perform a similar operation using the If/Then/Else format. Since I'm a tax accountant, I like to revert to tax examples for my macros. This time we'll create a macro called SingleTax that calculates U.S. individual income tax for a single individual, using the If/Then/Else macro style. In this way you'll see how you can nest several layers of If conditions within a single macro.

Here's a chart showing the 2008 U.S. income tax rates for a single individual:

- **10%** on income between $0 and $8,025

- **15%** on the income between $8,025 and $32,550; *plus* $802.50

- **25%** on the income between $32,550 and $78,850; *plus* $4,481.25

- **28%** on the income between $78,850 and $164,550; *plus* $16,056.25

- **33%** on the income between $164,550 and $357,700; *plus* $40,052.25

- **35%** on the income over $357,700; *plus* $103,791.75

Our macro must examine an income number, establish what income range the income amount falls in, and then calculate the appropriate income tax and place that amount in a cell.

It's easier to start this calculation at the top, the 35% tax rate, because then you can ask if the income is over a certain amount, whereas if you start at the bottom you have to determine if the income is within a certain range. You can structure the macro either way, but starting at the top results in fewer keystrokes.

We could follow the example set in the previous macro and have the macro examine the contents of a cell. Instead, let's use the techniques learned in Chapter 7, and use an `InputBox`. This way, we'll ask the worksheet user to enter the income to be analyzed, and then perform the tasks on the amount entered in the box.

The first portion of the code sets up the input box:

```
TaxableIncome = InputBox("Enter your taxable income")
If TaxableIncome > 357700 Then
        ActiveCell.Value = 103791.75 + (TaxableIncome - 357700) * 0.35
ElseIf TaxableIncome > 164550 Then
        ActiveCell.Value = 40052.25 + (TaxableIncome - 164550) * 0.33
ElseIf TaxableIncome > 78850 Then
        ActiveCell.Value = 16056.25 + (TaxableIncome - 78850) * 0.28
ElseIf TaxableIncome > 32550 Then
        ActiveCell.Value = 4481.25 + (TaxableIncome - 32550) * 0.25
ElseIf TaxableIncome > 8025 Then
        ActiveCell.Value = 802.50 + (TaxableIncome - 78850) * 0.15
ElseIf TaxableIncome > 0 Then
        ActiveCell.Value = TaxableIncome  * 0.10
End If
```

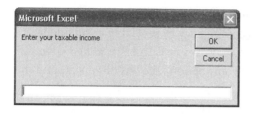

Figure 10-4   SingleTax macro uses an input box to request taxable income amount.

This macro gets placed between the Sub SingleTax() and End Sub lines, and you've got a complete macro. Test the macro by opening a worksheet and running the SingleTax macro. A dialog box like the one in Figure 10-4 appears, asking you to input your taxable income.

When you enter the amount of income and click OK, the correct income tax calculation appears in the currently active cell.

Create a Nested If/Then Macro

Sometimes one question isn't enough information to get you to the results you need. You can create a macro that asks more than one If question, and produce different layers of actions based on the answers.

For example, let's say we want to confirm that the taxable income used in the previous macro is really 2008 taxable income, so that the correct rates apply. Rather than just providing an input box that asks for the income, we can first ask for the income, and then ask for a confirmation that this is 2008 income. If the answer is Yes, the macro operation continues and the tax is calculated. If the answer is No, the macro execution stops and a message appears telling the user that tax rates for different years are not available.

The first line of the macro remains intact—the InputBox command asks the user for 2008 taxable income.

Next we need a new If statement, asking if this is really 2008 taxable income. The following code results in the message shown in Figure 10-5:

```
x = MsgBox("Is this your 2008 taxable income?", 3)
If x = 6 Then
```

MEMO

The message box codes (3 for a Yes/No box, and 6, which stands for the answer Yes) can be found in Chapter 7.

Next you insert all of the macro code from the original SingleTax macro. It is wise to indent this code so that you can keep track of your If statements and the related End If statement. Finally, you need

Figure 10-5   Revised macro asks user to confirm that he entered 2008 taxable income.

Figure 10-6 This message appears if the user indicates that 2008 income was not entered.

to provide for the possibility that the user did not enter a Yes answer in the message box. We'll take care of this contingency by providing an additional message box advising the user that the tax can't be calculated, as shown in Figure 10-6. If the user clicks OK (the only option), the box disappears and the macro operation ends.

```
Else
MsgBox ("Unable to calculate your income tax")
End If
```

The completed macro (named SingleTax2 to distinguish it from its predecessor) is shown in Figure 10-7.

156

```
PERSONAL.XLSB - Module10 (Code)

(General)                                      SingleTax2

Sub SingleTax2()
'
'Macro to calculate U.S. individual income tax for single taxpa
'
TaxableIncome = InputBox("Enter your taxable income")
x = MsgBox("Is this your 2008 taxable income?", 3)
If x = 6 Then

    If TaxableIncome > 357700 Then
        ActiveCell.Value = 103791.75 + (TaxableIncome - 357700)
    ElseIf TaxableIncome > 164550 Then
        ActiveCell.Value = 40052.25 + (TaxableIncome - 164550)
    ElseIf TaxableIncome > 78850 Then
        ActiveCell.Value = 16056.25 + (TaxableIncome - 78850)
    ElseIf TaxableIncome > 32550 Then
        ActiveCell.Value = 4481.25 + (TaxableIncome - 32550) *
    ElseIf TaxableIncome > 8025 Then
        ActiveCell.Value = 802.5 + (TaxableIncome - 78850) * 0.
    ElseIf TaxableIncome > 0 Then
        ActiveCell.Value = TaxableIncome * 0.1
    End If
Else
MsgBox ("Unable to calculate your income tax")
End If

End Sub
```

Figure 10-7 Complete code for the SingleTax2 macro

Exploring Loops

When you have a batch of data that needs processing, you often tell the computer to do something over and over. In programming, this repetitive behavior is called a *loop*. In real life, it's called a *job*.

Loops are useful in many different situations. Searching through 5,082 invoices for those that are overdue involves looping. Addressing 400 envelopes does too. In fact, computers are sometimes called *data processors*, and looping is a big part of the processing that goes on.

One of the most useful commands in VBA is For. It indicates the start of a commonly used loop structure. VBA repeatedly carries out the instructions between the For and its companion command, Next.

The number of times the computer will loop is specified by the two numbers listed following the For. Here's an example. See if you can guess the value of the variable X after this loop finishes executing:

```
Sub ExploreLoop
For I = 1 To 12
      X = X + 2
Next I
MsgBox X
End Sub
```

A loop has a *loop counter variable*, and in a For...Next loop, this variable is traditionally named I. Nobody is quite sure whether this I stands for *iteration* or *increment*. But the idea is that each time the loop executes, the value in I is automatically incremented (raised). Equally compelling is the idea that a loop iterates (repeats).

In any case, the first line of this loop translates: each time this loop executes, raise the value in the variable I by 1. When I finally reaches 12, the looping is complete and stops—execution continues with the code following the Next I. In this example, execution continues by displaying the message box.

In other words, loop 12 times; then stop looping and display the message box.

So, when this code runs, it performs the code inside the loop 12 times. In effect, 2 is added to the contents of X each time the loop executes. X starts with 0, but the first time through the loop X contains 2, and then the next time the loop runs it contains 4, then 6, and so on.

NEW WAYS TO TEST MACROS

When you run the macro with the message box inside the loop, you have to click the OK button 12 times. However, there's a way to exit a loop early: Press CTRL+BREAK. This puts you into *break mode*. A special message box is displayed, giving you three options:

- **Continue**   Resume execution.

- **End**   Exit the macro.

- **Debug**   Stay in break mode, where you can use debugging tools such as single-stepping through the code, or using the *Immediate Window* to check the value of variables. For example, click the Debug button in the break mode message box. Now press CTRL+G to display the Immediate Window. Type **?X** in the Immediate Window and press ENTER.

This means: display the value currently in the variable X. The value is displayed in the Immediate Window. Choose Run | Reset to stop execution (leaving break mode and returning to normal code-writing mode in the Editor).

While on the subject of the Immediate Window, it has another special use when you're writing code that involves loops or other repetitive behaviors: displaying results. Throughout this book, including here in this chapter, you've seen how to use the MsgBox command to help test macro code by showing you what's going on. But as illustrated in the second code example, it can be tedious to have to repeatedly click the OK button to move the code forward each time a message box is displayed within

NEW WAYS TO TEST MACROS (CONT.)

a loop. The solution is to print repetitive results in the Immediate Window rather than in a message box. Try executing this macro, and view the results in the Immediate Window:

```
Sub ExploreLoop()

For I = 1 To 12
    X = X + 2
    Debug.Print X
Next I
End Sub
```

If you wish, you can leave the Immediate Window open all the time while testing code. The Immediate Window behaves much like Notepad. For example, to clear the Immediate Window, just press CTRL+A to select all the contents, then press DELETE to delete.

The variable X is incremented 12 times (1 To 12), and each time 2 is added. So when this little macro runs, the message box displays 24 as the final value in X.

```
Sub ExploreLoop()

For I = 1 To 12
    X = X + 2
    MsgBox X
Next I
End Sub
```

The Three Kinds of For...Next Loops

You can specify the precise number of loops that are to be taken before moving past the For...Next structure (as we did in the code examples earlier in this chapter):

```
For I = 1 to 20
```

The second type of For...Next loop employs a variable (or expression) to specify the number of loops. Perhaps you want to allow the user to decide how many copies of a document should be printed. You display an input box

MEMO

Notice that if you add a semicolon to the end of the Debug .Print line, the results are printed horizontally within the Immediate Window rather than using up a separate line for each result. Also, if you're mystified by the Debug.Print command in general, see the briefing earlier in this chapter.

with the prompt "How Many Copies?" and after the user types in the number, you loop the number of times the variable specifies:

```
Sub ExploreLoop1()
NumberOfCopies = InputBox("How many copies")


For I = 1 To NumberOfCopies
    Debug.Print I;
Next I


End Sub
```

Stepping Through a Loop

The third variation on the For...Next loop involves skipping steps. There is an optional command that works with For...Next called Step. Step can be attached at the end of the For line to force VBA to skip loop iterations, to *step* past them. Step alters the way a loop counts.

As you've seen, a loop normally counts by one:

```
For I = 1 to 12
    Debug.Print I;
Next I
```

Results in: 1 2 3 4 5 6 7 8 9 10 11 12

However, when you use the Step command, you can specify that the loop count every other number (by using Step 2):

```
For I = 1 to 12 Step 2
    Debug.Print I
Next I
```

Results in: 1 3 5 7 9 11

Or you could step every 15th number (Step 15):

```
For I = 15 to 90 Step 15
    Debug.Print I;
Next I
```

Results in: 15 30 45 60 75 90

MEMO

Additional variations using the Step command include *counting down backward* using a negative step (For I = 10 To 1 Step -1), and even counting by fractions (Step .25).

160

Nesting Loops

For...Next loops can also be *nested*, one inside the other. At first this sort of structure seems confusing, and it often actually is. But just do what most programmers do when perplexed: *hack*. The term *hacking* has several meanings in computing, but one meaning is: trying various approaches to see which one works. With nested loops, you can try various numbers for the counter variables, and try moving commands around in the "inner" or "outer" loop, to eventually figure out how to get the results you're after.

Nested loops can be confusing because you add a new dimension when you use an interior loop. The inner loop interacts with the exterior loop in ways that are immediately clear only to the mathematically gifted. Essentially, the inner loop does its thing the number of times specified by its own counter variable, *multiplied by* the counter variable of the outer loop.

In this situation, simply *hack* away until things work the way they should. *Hacking* to a programmer means precisely the same thing as carving to a sculptor—chipping away until the desired shape emerges. Notice in the following example we use a plain Debug.Print command (with no variable) in the outer loop. This has the effect of moving us down one line in the Immediate Window. This makes it easier to visualize the activity of the two loops:

```
For I = 1 to 5
     For J = 1 to 10
          Debug.Print I;
     Next J

     Debug.Print
Next I
```

Results in:

```
1 1 1 1 1 1 1 1 1 1
2 2 2 2 2 2 2 2 2 2
3 3 3 3 3 3 3 3 3 3
4 4 4 4 4 4 4 4 4 4
5 5 5 5 5 5 5 5 5 5
```

Note that you can start a loop's counter variable anywhere; you need not start the counter with 1. And the Step size can be whatever you wish, including negative numbers if you want to count *down* instead of up.

```
For I = 10 To 1 Step - 2
     Debug.Print I;
Next I
```

Results in: 10 8 6 4 2

Any *numeric expression* can be used with For...Next. (See Chapter 9 for a definition of *expression*.) However, the range you're counting must be *possible*. The following range is not possible:

```
For I = -10 To -20 Step 2
     Debug.Print "loop"; I
Next
```

This loop does nothing when you execute it. It cannot. You're asking it to count downward, but your Step command is positive. As any intelligent entity would when confronted with a senseless request, VBA does nothing with these instructions. It ignores you. To make this loop actually loop, you have to make the Step negative with –2:

```
For I = -10 To -20 Step -2
     Debug.Print "loop"; I
Next
```

Avoiding the Dreaded Endless Loop

Here are some additional notes about looping.

For...Next loop structures can be as large as you need them to be—they can contain as many lines of code between the For and the Next as you want. On the other hand, you can put a small For...Next structure all on one line, if you wish, by separating the "lines of code" using colons:

```
For J = 1 To 5: Debug.Print J: Next J
```

And that final J is optional, but omitting it makes your program slightly less easily understood. The following example illustrates how you can leave out the final variable name. This practice is frowned upon by some programming teachers (though it's actually quite frequently found in real-life programming):

```
For J = 1 To 5: Debug.Print J: Next
```

Now we come to the famous *endless loop*. Also known as an infinite loop, such a structure has no way of stopping. You have provided no exit, no condition that will allow the loop to finish. Here's one example:

```
Sub NoEndLoop()
For J = 1 To 5
    J = 3
Next J
End Sub
```

When you execute this, the only way to stop it is to press CTRL+BREAK if you're running it in the VB Editor, or press BREAK if it's been launched from within Excel as a macro.

Perhaps you see the problem here. The computer is attempting to finish an unfinishable job. Each time through this loop you reset the counter variable J to 3, so J never has a chance to reach 5 and thereby continues executing code below the loop structure (in this case the End Sub).

If you use Step 0, you will also create a loop that never ends. In effect, an endless loop causes the computer to go into a state of suspended animation.

There are some situations where you *do* want an endless loop, such as those continually repeating product demonstrations you see in stores. But these situations are rare. Endless loops are usually just a bug that you need to fix. Endless loops are even more common in other loop structures, such as Do...Loop, which we'll explore next.

Do...Loop: Repeat Until a Condition Is Met

An alternative to `For...Next` is a `Do...Loop`. This type of loop doesn't use a specified counter. It instead contains a condition that specifies when the loop is supposed to end. Although `For...Next` is the more common loop structure in programming, `Do...Loop` is the more flexible structure.

The reason that `For...Next` is used so often is that when you're writing your program, you often know how many times you want something done. So you can provide the counter variable with its exit condition.

As a generalization, when you want something done repeatedly but don't know the number of times you want it repeated, use a `Do...Loop` instead of a `For...Next` loop.

`For...Next` is good when you do know the number of times something should be done. `Do...Loop` is good when you know a condition that must be satisfied rather than the precise number of times a task should be performed.

Here's an illustration:

`For...Next` means: "Brush your hair 150 times."
`Do...Loop` means: "Brush your hair until it shines."

The flexibility of `Do...Loop` structures results from the variety of ways you can set up interior tests that exit the loop. Here's a simple example:

```
Do While x < 14
    x = x + 2
    Debug.Print x
Loop
```

Results in: 2 4 6 8 10 12 14

It's pretty easy to read this code. It means, do this looping as long as the value in variable x is less than 14. Once that condition is met, exit the loop and continue on with whatever code follows the `Loop`.

The Four Flavors of Do...Loops

`Do...Loops` come in four flavors. The first is illustrated in the following code example:

```
Do While x < 66
Loop
```

The second uses an `Until` command, like this:

```
Do Until x < 66
Loop
```

The difference between this `Until` version and the `While` version is that `Until` loops only as long as the condition *is false.* In other words, loop *until* x is less than 66. (As opposed to looping as long as the condition remains *true*: loop *while* x is less than 66.)

Actually, these two variations are pretty much interchangeable. It's just a matter of how you want to express things, like the difference between "Sweep *until* the porch is clean" versus "Sweep *while* the porch is dirty." The computer doesn't care about such things. However, expressing the condition in a particular way can sometimes make your meaning clearer to you and other humans who read your program.

Moving the Exit Condition to the End of the Loop Structure

The third and fourth variations of `Do...Loop` test the condition at the *end* instead of the beginning of the loop. This ensures that the loop *will always execute at least once.*

If you put the test condition at the start of the loop and the test fails, the loop will never execute even once. VBA will skip over the commands within the loop.

So, if you want a loop to always execute at least once, put the condition test at the bottom of the loop, like this:

```
Do
     Y = Y + 1
     Debug.Print Y
Loop Until Y >= 0
```

Results in: 1

But put the test Y >= 0 back up at the top of the loop and nothing is printed. Nothing happens because this loop won't even execute once. Y is not greater than or equal to zero at the start of this loop structure. So the loop immediately exits itself without carrying out any instructions within the loop, including the Debug.Print instruction:

```
Do Until Y >= 0
     Y = Y + 1
     Debug.Print Y
Loop
```

Results in:

While...Wend, a Less Powerful Do...Loop

Another variation on loop structures is While...Wend. This structure merely continues looping while a condition remains true. To loop as long as X is less than 24, you would write:

```
While X < 24: X = X + 1: Debug.Print X: Wend
```

While...Wend has no exit command. You can move past For...Next structures or Do...Loop structures using Exit For and Exit Do commands. But While...Wend has no such forced exit command.

Also, While...Wend is limited to testing the condition at the start of its loop structure.

Managing Object Collections with For Each...Next Loops

VBA itself manages the exit condition in a special kind of loop structure called For Each...Next. You can use For Each...Next with an array, because VBA knows how big the array is, so VBA knows when to exit the loop.

In other words, with the For Each...Next structure, you don't use a counter variable, or specify an exit condition, as you do with For...Next and Do...Loop structures.

Here's an example:

```
Sub ForEachTest()
Dim MyNames(1 To 6)

For I = 1 To 6
      MyNames(I) = "Name" & I
Next I

For Each Thing In MyNames
      Debug.Print Thing
 Next

End Sub
```

Results in: Name1 Name2 Name3 Name4 Name5 Name6

In this code you first declare an array called MyNames. You specify that this array holds six items. Then you use a traditional For...Next loop to store six strings (Name1, Name2, and so on) in this array.

But when you go to print the contents of this array, you use the For...Each structure to iterate through the array. When VBA reaches the upper boundary of the array (index item 6), it automatically exits the For...Each loop. Notice that I used a variable named Thing, but you can use any variable name you want in the For...Each loop. However, the variable must be of the variant or object type (if you don't specify a variable's type, VBA automatically makes it a variant, as in the above example).

For...Each is typically used with *collections*—a set of objects. You can create your own collections, like this:

```
Sub MakeCollection()

Dim MyNames As New Collection
For I = 1 To 20
    MyNames.Add "Name" & I
Next I

For Each Thing In MyNames
    Debug.Print Thing
Next

End Sub
```

You can use the Add method to fill a collection with data, then use For...Each to iterate through your collection. There are also built-in collections, such as the Sheets collection that contains all worksheets (and charts) in the currently active (or selected) workbook. Here's an example that employs the UsedRange method to display all the data in a worksheet:

```
Sub SeeCollection()
    Dim r As Range
    For Each r In ActiveSheet.UsedRange
        Debug.Print r.Value
    Next
End Sub
```

Here you create a variable of the Range type, and then use it to access each cell in the currently active sheet's "used range" (the cells contained within an imaginary rectangle drawn around all cells that contain actual data). Try this code. You'll see how this technique can be a very quick way to search through a worksheet (to modify cells that meet a particular criterion, or to find, for example, any cells that contain 33):

```
For Each r In ActiveSheet.UsedRange
        If r = 33 Then
```

```
                              Debug.Print r.Value
                     End If
             Next
```

The following example illustrates how to use the address property of the range object to identify which cells contain the value 33:

```
Sub SeeCollection()
    Dim r As Range
    For Each r In ActiveSheet.UsedRange
        If r = 33 Then
            Debug.Print r.Address & ": ";
            Debug.Print r.Value
            Debug.Print 'move down one line in the Immediate Window
        End If
    Next
End Sub
```

TAKE A LOOK AT EXCEL'S OBJECTS AND COLLECTIONS

Excel, like the other Office applications, contains many built-in collections you can employ in your programming. To see the various objects and collections that are built into Excel, follow these steps:

1. From the main Excel window, press ALT+F11 to get to the VB Editor.

2. In the Editor, choose Help | Microsoft Visual Basic Help | MSDN on the Web.

    You'll see a web page with a Live Search field.

3. Type **Excel 2007 object model map** into the search field.

    A list of links appears.

4. In the list of links, click *Excel Object Model Reference* (or *Excel 2007 object model map*).

5. It may also be necessary to click an additional link: *Excel Object Model Map*.

In any case, what you're looking for can be found by pasting this address into your Internet browser:

```
http://msdn2.microsoft.com/en-us/
library/bb332345.aspx
```

You'll now be able to examine the object model, as shown in Figure 11-1. Objects are shown in blue; collections in yellow.

You can click any of the objects or collections displayed in the object model map to open a Help screen describing how to use that object or collection. In fact, you'll frequently find good code examples that you can copy and paste into the VB Editor to explore, or modify for use in your own macros.

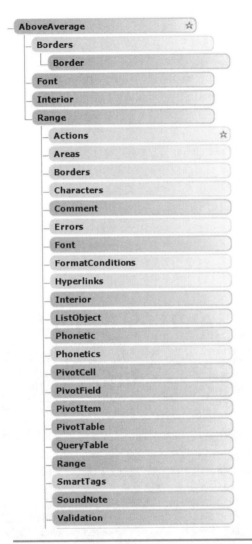

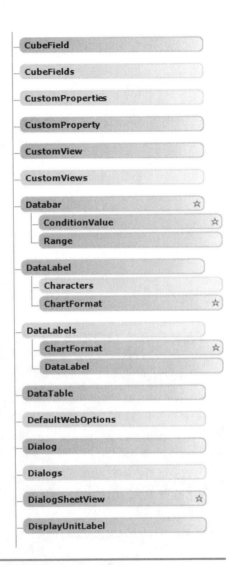

170

Figure 11-1   Excel has dozens of built-in collections you can manipulate, as shown in this object model map.

Adding Controls to Your Worksheets

You can execute macros in several ways:

- Create a keyboard shortcut such as ALT+F.

- Add a button to the Quick Access toolbar.

- Press ALT+F8 to bring up the Macros dialog box.

- Press F5 while in the VB Editor (after clicking within the macro to place the blinking insertion cursor in the macro).

- Put a control, such as a button, on a worksheet that the user can interact with.

It's this last method that we'll explore in this chapter. You'll see how to add controls to your worksheets to make it easier for people to execute your macros. Clicking a button or other control that's sitting right there on a worksheet has to be about the fastest, most intuitive way to execute code.

Recall from the section "Creating Custom Dialogs" in Chapter 7 that you can create a custom dialog box by adding controls from the Toolbox in the VBA Editor. Then you write some code in an *event handler* such as a Click event. This approach is quite similar to writing a macro, except event handler code executes when the user clicks the control.

MEMO

If you prefer, you can just click to place the button, but dragging gives you control over the size and shape. You can always reposition or reshape a control by clicking it to select it, then either dragging it as a whole to move it, or dragging one of the eight small "handles" on the control's sides to resize it.

THE EASY WAY

If you want to clone a control—so you can be sure that a new control will be the same size and shape as the original—just click to select the control, press CTRL+C to copy it, then press CTRL+V to make a copy, or multiple copies.

You can put controls on worksheets, and write code to make things happen when the user clicks (or otherwise interacts) with the controls. Let's see how it's done.

Using Buttons to Execute Code

In this example, we'll assume that you frequently find yourself zooming in to view selected cells, then zooming back out to normal view. So, instead of zooming by using tabs, using the zoom slider in the bottom right of the worksheet window, or clicking icons, try putting a couple of buttons right on your worksheet instead. Click one to zoom in; click the other to return to normal view.

Adding Buttons to a Worksheet

To add a button to a worksheet, follow these steps:

1. Click the Developer tab on the Ribbon.

2. Click the Insert icon to display the available controls, as shown in Figures 12-1 and 12-2.

3. Click the ActiveX Command Button icon as shown in Figure 12-2.

   Two things happen when you click the button icon: The Design Mode icon is enabled (turns gold) and your mouse pointer changes into a crosshairs. The Design Mode icon on the Ribbon means you can't interact normally with the worksheet—instead you're able to position and resize controls, and also, as you'll see, write code for those controls. To return to normal worksheet interaction at any time, just click the Design Mode icon. It will be disabled.

4. With your mouse, drag somewhere on the worksheet to create a button, as shown in Figure 12-1.

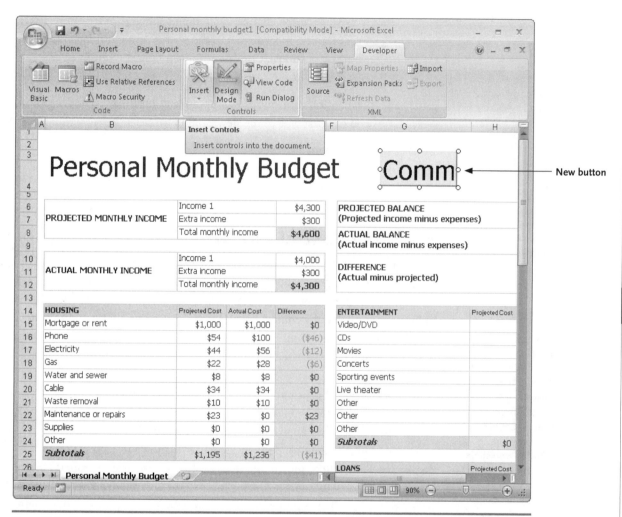

Figure 12-1   Use the Insert icon to add controls to a worksheet.

5. Click the button to select it, then press CTRL+C to copy it.

6. Press CTRL+V to paste a new, clone button. Drag the clone so it's next to the original.

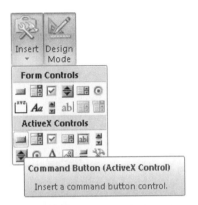

Figure 12-2 Click on the first ActiveX control button, the Command Button.

7. Now you want to change the default caption (CommandButton1) to something meaningful to the user. Right-click the first button and choose CommandButton Object | Edit from the context menu.

8. The button control is now framed with hashmarks. At this point you can just type in the new caption.

9. Type **Zoom** as the caption for the button on the left, and repeat steps 7 and 8 to change the caption on the right button to **UnZoom** (see Figure 12-3).

Figure 12-3 When you choose the Edit option, you can directly type in a button's caption.

Adjusting Control Properties

Now you may want to change the appearance or otherwise modify some of the properties of your new button controls.

Click one of the buttons to select it *alone*. (If the buttons are grouped, then ungroup them using the context menu's Grouping option. If the buttons are both selected, unselect them by clicking elsewhere in the worksheet. You want only one button to be selected because that's the only way to bring up the Properties window.)

Right-click one of your buttons to display its context menu, then choose Properties (or click the Properties item in the Controls section of the Ribbon). The Properties window appears, as shown in Figure 12-4.

Double-click the Font property in the window shown in Figure 12-4 to display the Font dialog, shown on the right. Change the Name property in the Properties window to **ZoomIt** (for the button that is captioned Zoom). This Name property will also automatically become the name of the sub (the event handler where you write your code to make things happen when this button is clicked).

Double-click the Font property in the window shown in Figure 12-4, to display the font dialog, shown on the right. Change the Name property in the Properties window to ZoomIt (for the button that is captioned Zoom).

MEMO

If you want to reposition two or more controls as a unit, hold down the CTRL key as you click each control. This creates a group of controls you can now drag around the worksheet and drop to a new location—as a group. In this mode, you can also right-click one of the grouped controls, choose Format Control from the context menu, and adjust several properties including size.

UNDERSTANDING THE TWO SETS OF CONTROLS

I'm sure you couldn't help but notice the strange shadow set of controls—nearly duplicates of the ActiveX set—shown in Figure 12-2. This second set is titled *form controls* and we've been avoiding dealing with them in this chapter. Why? Because they are less flexible and less useful than their ActiveX counterparts. They're compatible with earlier versions of Excel, but are somewhat harder to work with, have few properties, can't trigger events, and generally allow you less freedom. So, my suggestion is that you avoid them in favor of the ActiveX set of controls.

However, there are a few situations where you might want to use a form control. ActiveX controls require that you create an event handler (such as `Button_Click`), but the older form controls can directly trigger macros. This isn't much of a difference really (you can just copy code from an existing macro and paste it into an event handler). But if you want to do something really simple and quick, like add a button that just executes an existing macro, go ahead and use a form control button if you wish.

You can't select form controls by clicking the Design Mode button. It has no effect on them. Instead, right-click it to select it. And you assign a macro to it by right-clicking, then choosing Assign Macro from the context menu. A list of your macros appears.

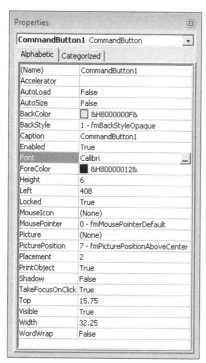

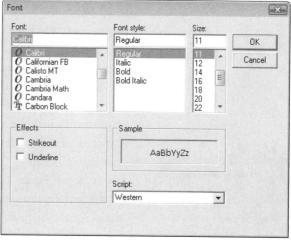

Figure 12-4   You can change many of the qualities of a control in its Properties window.

This Name property will also automatically become the name of the sub (the event handler where you write your code to make things happen when this button is clicked). Also change the font size to something that looks good to you.

Now click the other button to select it. Notice how the Properties window changes to display the properties of this newly selected control. Repeat the above steps to change the Name property of the second button to **UnZoomIt**, and the font size to match the other button.

If you wish, muck about with the colors and so on. Such things are a matter of personal taste, or the lack thereof. You can even add a picture using the Picture property, which can be kind of cool.

Now close the Properties window. You're ready to add the code.

Writing Code for Buttons and Other Controls

OK. You've got some pretty buttons up there on the worksheet, but what's beauty without the ability to do some job? Well, in some cases, beauty is its own justification. But we want these buttons to do some work.

Double-click the button captioned *Zoom*. The VB Editor opens up, displaying the `Click` event handler for the button named *ZoomIt*. (If the Editor doesn't open, you've deselected the Design Mode icon in the Ribbon's Developer tab. Select it and try again.)

The `ZoomIt_Click` that you see in Figure 12-5 handles the `Click` event (responds when the user clicks) for this button named ZoomIt. In other words, it's just like a macro, but instead of executing via a shortcut key combination or some other trigger, this code executes when the user clicks this particular button.

Also notice in Figure 12-5 that this `Button_Click` event handler is stored within (and thus is available to) this particular worksheet only. This restricted, local availability makes sense because this button is located only on this worksheet. The code is not in the Personal project (that would make it available to all current and future worksheets).

We want to make the Zoom button blow up any selected area on the worksheet. If nothing is selected, the whole thing blows up.

176

MEMO

As you learned earlier in this book, to find out what code you need to insert in this event handler, you can just record a macro performing the actions you want the event handler to carry out.

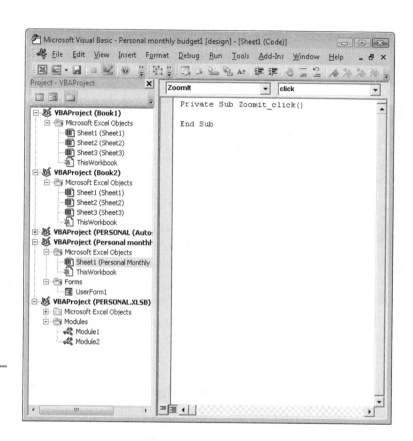

Figure 12-5 You use the VB Editor to write code for event handlers like this button's `Click` event.

MEMO

A click is an *event*—but most controls have additional events. You can see a list of these events by dropping down the list box in the upper-right side of the VB Editor when you're writing code for an event handler.

Type the following line into the `Click` event:

```
Private Sub ZoomIt_Click()
    ActiveWindow.Zoom = True
End Sub
```

Now go back to the worksheet, click the Developer tab, and deselect the Design Mode icon. This way you can test your new button. Click the Zoom button. Try it with some cells selected. To return to normal view, click the 100% icon in the Ribbon's View tab.

To program your UnZoom button, select the Design Mode icon, then double-click the UnZoom button to open its `Click` event handler. Type the following line into the `UnZoomIt_Click()` event:

```
Private Sub UnZoomIt_Click()
    ActiveWindow.Zoom = 100
End Sub
```

Now you can both zoom, and restore normal view, via your two buttons.

Exploring Other Controls

You'll find various other controls available when you click the Insert icon in the Ribbon's Developer tab. Let's look at several of these controls and see what they do and when they're appropriate.

Toggle button controls are useful for situations similar to light-switch behavior: two states, the lights are on or off. That's similar to what you've been doing with the zoom feature you added to your worksheet in this chapter. It might be more efficient to replace the two zooming buttons with just a toggle button. When clicked, it zooms. When clicked a second time, it unzooms.

Adding a Toggle Button

Let's give it a try. Click the Design Mode icon to enable that mode. Click your custom Zoom button to select it, then press DELETE to get rid of the button. Likewise, select and delete your UnZoom button. Deleting these controls doesn't destroy the event handler code in the VB Editor, which we'll reuse for our new toggle button.

Now add an ActiveX toggle button by clicking the Insert icon next to the Design Mode icon, then selecting the toggle button and either dragging it or just clicking to place it on a worksheet.

Double-click the new toggle button to open the VB Editor, and then type this into the toggle button's `Click` event:

```
Private Sub ToggleButton1_Click()
Static Clicked As Boolean
Clicked = Not Clicked

If Clicked Then
    ActiveWindow.Zoom = True
Else
    ActiveWindow.Zoom = 100
End If

End Sub
```

This code deserves some explanation. The `Static` command is quite useful in situations like this, so you should have it in your programmer's bag of tricks. `Static` preserves variables. When a variable is declared `Static` (as opposed to using the `Dim` command described in the briefing in Chapter 9), that variable and the value it holds are retained. An ordinary, nonstatic variable is destroyed along with its contents whenever a macro or event handler finishes execution. But we want to preserve the value in our variable named `Clicked` because that tells us the current status of the toggle button.

Here's what happens, step by step, in this code.

1. We declare a static (nonvolatile) variable named `Clicked`. And we specify that it's a Boolean variable type.

2. By writing `Clicked = Not Clicked`, we switch the value in `Clicked` to its opposite. In other words, if `Clicked` contained `False`, it now contains `True`. A Boolean variable can contain only two possible values, `True` or `False`. This makes it ideal for a toggle situation. Every time the line of code `Clicked = Not Clicked` executes, it changes from `False` to `True`, or `True` to `False`. In other words, this Boolean variable behaves just like a light switch, or

for that matter, like a toggle button control. What's more, this variable is `Static`, so it remembers its contents even when the event handler code is finished executing.

3. The rest of the code is easily understood, once you see how a static Boolean variable switches between two states when you use the `Not` command. `If Clicked` means "if the variable named `Clicked` is holding the value of `True`." So, if it is holding the value of `True`, the user has clicked that button (the button looks as if it's been sunk into the worksheet, indicating that it's "on" or "active"). We therefore want to zoom in response to this click:

    ```
    ActiveWindow.Zoom = True
    ```

    But, if this is the user's second time clicking this button, they're turning the zoom off. So the `Else` section of the `If...Then` structure is triggered, and this code executes to restore normal view:

    ```
    ActiveWindow.Zoom = 100
    ```

Using a Spin Button

The spin button control has an up arrow and a down arrow. It's two buttons in one. Typically, spin buttons are used to increase or decrease something. We'll use it to increase or decrease the zoom level each time the user clicks it. Click the up arrow and zoom increases. The down arrow, and it decreases.

Let's see how we can use a spin button to let the user adjust the zoom percent. Add a spin button to your spreadsheet, and also add a label control.

You might think we'll have to use a `Static` variable in this code to remember the current zoom value, but you'd be wrong. You can access many controls' properties during VBA code execution. And this spin button control has a `value` property that goes up by 1 each time the up arrow is clicked, and down by 1 each time the down arrow is clicked. And this `value` is retained until you close the worksheet on which it resides.

The `value` property of the spin button starts at zero. But we know that the minimum zoom factor for a worksheet is 100 (meaning 100 percent).

And the maximum zoom is 400. So we don't want to allow the user to click outside these values. We're going to use the value property and multiply it by 100 to set the zoom. So we'll want a value of 1, 2, 3, or 4. We don't want to allow the user to go below 1 or above 4 in their clicking (that would cause an error and would halt the code execution).

You could write code that checked these boundaries (> 0 and < 5) and enforced them in your event handler. But that's cumbersome and, in this case, checking for what programmers call *boundary conditions* simply isn't necessary. Luckily for us, the spin button control has a pair of built-in properties that will limit its range. So, right-click the spin button control and choose Properties from the context menu to open its Properties window. Set the Min property to 1 and the Max property to 4.

Right-click the label and choose Properties from the context menu (if the Properties window is still visible, you can just click the label control to select it and the Properties window will automatically switch to display the label's properties). Change the label's caption property to: **Click to zoom.**

Now double-click the spin button to open its code window.

```
Private Sub SpinButton1_Change()

v = SpinButton1.Value
ActiveWindow.Zoom = 100 * v
End Sub
```

In this code, you access a property of the spin button three times. First you *read* (obtain) the value currently in the value property of SpinButton1. Notice how you must specify the control's name, separated by a period (.) from the property whose data you want to see.

So, after the first line of code executes, the variable v contains whatever is in the value property of this particular spin button. Remember that the button's Max and Min properties prevent the values from going below 1 or above 4. Then all you have to do is set the zoom property to 100 times the spin button's current value. This results in four possible zoom values: 100, 200, 300, and 400.

181

Index

Note: Page numbers referencing figures are italicized and followed by an "*f*."

2008 U.S. Corporate
Income Tax Rates, 97*f*,
153–154

A

absolute references, 8
Activate events, 115
ActiveCell command, 25
ActiveCell.CurrentRegion
.Select command, 131
ActiveX CommandButton
icon, 172, 174*f*
ActiveX controls, 174*f*, 175
ActiveX toggle buttons, 178
Add method, 168
Alphabetic tab, 22
apostrophes, 24–25, 46–47
argument lists, 84
arguments, 24, 104–105
arithmetic operators, 139
arrays
    numbers versus
      names, 143–145
    overview, 142–143
    rules, 145–146

Auto Quick Info feature,
105*f*, 106

B

Bonus function, 101–102
Boolean variables, 179–180
boundary conditions, 181
break mode, 89, 158
built-in constants, 111
Button_Click event
handler, 176, 178
buttons
    adding worksheets to,
      172–174
    toolbar, 67, 69
    writing code for,
      176–178
Buttons argument, 109–110

C

Cancel buttons, 113–114
capitalization, 135
case sensitivity, 135
Categorized tab, 22

cells, formatting. *See*
    formatting, cells
Cells command, 131
center alignment,
    31–34, 123
Choose Commands From
    drop-down menu, 68–69
Click event handler,
    176–177
code
    for cell formatting,
      32–33
    copying and
      pasting, 48
    examples of, 76
    familiarization
      with, 31
    harvesting
      constructing
        macros, 45–50
      modules, 45
      overview, 44–45
      removing old
        macros, 50–51
      testing
        macros, 50

code (*cont.*)
    paring, 78–80
    viewing, 38–40
    writing
        for buttons and
            controls,
            176–178
        for input boxes,
            106–108
        for macros, 78
Code group, 20
Code window, 22–23,
    75, 107
collections, 168–169
colons, 92
color palette, 129
Column Width dialog
    box, 43
columns, 42–43, 49, 127
Comma style, 125
CommandButton control,
    113–114
commands
    date and time, 83–84
    error, 87–88
    financial calculation,
        85–87
    finding arguments
        for, 106
    math, 84–85
    by name
        ActiveCell, 25
        ActiveCell
        .CurrentRegion
            .Select, 131
        Cells, 131
        CurrentRegion,
            132

DateDiff, 84
Debug.Print,
    160–162
Dim, 108, 136,
    145–146, 179
Dimension, 129
End Sub, 26, 46
Exit Sub, 87
Format, 83, 87
FormulaR1C1, 25
GoSub, 92
If...Then, 107
InputBox,
    104–106, 154
InStr, 82
LCase, 83
Left, 83
Mid, 82
MsgBox,
    84, 109
Offset, 27
Paste Special, 39
Range, 26,
    131–132
Replace, 83
Round, 84–85
Select, 26–27
Selection, 132
Static, 179–180
Step, 160, 162
Until, 165
View Macros, 68
While, 165
With...End With,
    47–49
With Selection,
    78, 123–124

text manipulation,
    81–83
understandability
    of, 80
VB Editor, 88–89
writing
    overview, 74–80
    paring code,
        78–80
    understanding
        code, 78
commas, 104
comment lines, 46–47
comparison operators,
    138–139
conditional expressions,
    148–149
constants, built-in, 111
controls
    adjusting properties,
        174–176
    writing code for,
        176–178
copying
    code, 130
    controls, 172
    macros, 46, 58–59
corporate income tax
    calculations, 97–101,
        153–155
CorpTax function,
    98–101
counting down
    backward, 160
current workbook, 15–16,
    56–57
CurrentRegion
    command, 132

customization
    date, 120–121
    dialog
        adding items
           to List Box,
           114–116
        offering list
           of options,
           112–114
        responding to
           user selection,
           116–117
    function
        hiding sensitive
           data, 101–102
        simplifying
           complicated
           calculations,
           97–101
    toolbar, 66–70, 71f
Customize Quick Access
    Toolbar drop-down list,
    69–70

D

data processors, 157
date and time commands,
    83–84
date macros, 10–12
date options, 120–121
DateDiff command, 84
datum, variable, 134–135
Debug menu, 89
Debug.Print command,
    160–162
Default argument,
    104–105

default dates, 120
Delete button, 51
Description field, 5
Design Mode icon, 172
Developer Ribbon, 20
Dim command, 108, 136,
    145–146, 179
Dimension command, 129
dimensions, array, 145
Do...Loop
    moving exit condition
        to end of, 165–166
    overview, 164–165
    While...Wend
        structure, 166

E

Edit menu, 88
Edit option, 174
editing macros
    saving edited
        macros, 29
    in VB Editor
        Code window,
           22–23
        modules, 21
        Project Explorer,
           20–21
        Properties
           window, 21–22
Else operation, 148, 151
ElseIf operation, 152–153
enabling macros, 58–59
End Sub command,
    26, 46
endless loops, 162–163
error handlers, 87–88

error messages, 135
event handlers, 115,
    176–177
Excel Developer Reference
    material, 31
Excel keyboard shortcuts,
    63–65
Excel Options window,
    3–4, 67–69
Exit Sub command, 87
expressions, 137–138, 161

F

file extensions, 56
File menu, 88
files, macro-enabled, 56
financial calculations
    commands, 85–87
font selection, 124, 127
For Each...Next loops,
    167–170
form controls, 175
formal variable
    declaration, 136
Format command, 83, 87
Format menu, 89
formatting
    cells
        changing
           existing
           formats,
           120–121
        color scheme,
           128–129
        column
           headings,
           122–124

formatting (*cont.*)
  formatting macros, 129–131
  number appearance, 125–126
  overview, 12–14, 126–128
  VBA commands, 131–132
macros, 55–56, 96–97, 129–131
Formula bar, 36–37
FormulaR1C1 command, 25
formulas, displaying as values
  overview, 36–40
  testing macros, 38
  viewing macro code, 38–40
For...Next loops
  endless, 162–163
  nesting, 161–162
  Step command, 160
fractions, 160
function arguments, 102*f*
Function Arguments window, 100
functions, customized
  hiding sensitive data, 101–102
  simplifying complicated calculations, 97–101

G

GoSub command, 92
gridlines, 41, 127
grouped buttons, 174

H

hacking, 161
hard-coding, 105
hard-wiring, 105
harvesting code
  constructing new macros, 45–50
  modules, 45
  overview, 44–51
  removing old macros, 50–51
  testing macros, 50
Help field, 30
Help system, 29–34, 76, 81
hidden workbooks, 51–52
horizontal alignment, 31–32

I

I variable, 158
If...Then command, 107
If/Then/Else macros
  calling subroutines, 93–94
  Else operation, 151
  ElseIf operation, 152–153
  If/Then macros
    nested, 155–156
    simple, 149–150

multilevel, 153–155
  overview, 147–148
Immediate Window, 158–159
implicit declaration, 136
Income Tax Rates, 2008 U.S. Corporate, 97*f*, 153–154
increments, 158
index numbers, 144–145
infinite loops, 163
input boxes
  writing and testing code for, 106–108
  writing complete macros, 106
InputBox command, 93–95, 104–108, 154
Insert Function dialog box, 99–100
Insert icon, 172, 173*f*
InStr command, 82
integer division, 84
interactive macros
  arguments, 104–105
  custom dialogs
    adding items to List Box, 114–116
    offering user list of options, 112–114
    responding to user's selection, 116–117

input boxes
  writing and testing code for, 106–108
  writing complete macros, 106
message boxes, 109–111
interest rate calculations, 85–87
iteration, 158

K

keyboard shortcuts, 61–65

L

labels, 92–93
Landscape option, 42, 48
LCase command, 83
Left command, 83
ListItem property, 116
literals, 137
Lock Project for Viewing checkbox, 60
logical operators, 140
loop counter variables, 158
loops
  Do...Loop
    moving exit condition to end of, 165–166
    overview, 164–165
    While...Wend structure, 166

For Each...Next, 167–170
For...Next
  endless, 162–163
  nesting, 161–162
  Step command, 160
  overview, 157–158
  testing macros, 158–159

M

Macro button, 6, 43
macro code. *See* code
macro commands. *See* commands
Macro Name field, 5, 51
Macro Options dialog box, 61–62
Macro Recorder, 14, 43, 121
macro-enabled files, 56
macro-enabled workbooks, 15, 17
math operations, 84–85
message boxes, 109–111, 155–156
Mid command, 82
Mod operator, 139
Modify Button window, 69
modules, 21, 45
monthly reports, 12–13
MsgBox command, 84, 109
multilevel If/Then/Else macros, 153–155

N

NAME1 macro
  command lines, 25–26
  comment lines, 25
  overview, 24–26
  testing, 6–7
NAME2 macro, 8, 26–27
NAME3 macro, 9–10, 27–28
names
  of functions, 98
  of macros, 28
  of modules, 57–58
  versus numbers, 143–145
  of subroutines, 92–93
  of variables, 135
nested If/Then macros, 155–156
nesting loops, 161–162
numbers
  of items, 117
  versus names, 143–145
numeric expressions, 161

O

Object Browser, 28–29
object model map, 169, 170*f*
objects, 28, 31, 169
Offset command, 27
offsets, 150
OK buttons, 113–114
operator precedence, 141–142

operators
    arithmetic, 139
    comparison, 139
    logical, 140
    overview, 138
    string, 140
optional arguments, 105
orientation, page, 42, 48

P

Page Layout ribbon, 41
page orientation, 42, 48
parentheses, 24, 98–99,
    104, 141–142
paring code, 78–80
passwords, 60
Paste Special command, 39
Personal Macro Workbook
    deleting macros from,
        51–52
    saving macros to, 15,
        55, 75
Print Gridlines feature,
    41–42
Project Explorer, 20–21
Project Explorer window,
    44, 74, 115
Project Properties
    window, 60
Prompt argument,
    104–105
Properties window
    adjusting control
        properties, 174–176

changing module
    names in, 108
opening, 57
overview, 21–22, 75
protecting macros, 59–60
Protection tab, 60

Q

Quick Access toolbar,
    66–70
Quick Info option, 28

R

Range command, 26,
    131–132
reading macros
    NAME1
        command lines,
            25–26
        comment
            lines, 25
        overview, 24–26
    NAME2, 26–27
    NAME3, 27–28
Record Macro dialog box
    overview, 5
    recording date
        macros in, 11
    Shortcut Key field,
        61–62
    Store Macro In list
        box, 75
recording macros
    Developer ribbon, 2–4

formatting with
    macros, 12–14
overview, 40–43
reading macros
    NAME1, 4–7
    NAME2, 7–8
    NAME3, 8–10
saving macros
    to current
        workbook,
        15–16
    to new
        workbook,
        16–17
    to Personal
        Macro
        Workbook, 15,
        55, 75
    simple date macros,
        10–12
references, 8, 149
Relative References
    feature, 8, 149
renaming modules,
    57–58
Replace command, 83
returned values, 110*f*
Round command,
    84–85
Run menu, 89

S

Save As window, 15–16
saving
    changes, 34, 52

macros
  to current workbook, 15–16
  editing, 29
  to new workbook, 16–17
  to Personal Macro Workbook, 15, 55, 75
  workbooks, 55
Select Case statement, 98
Select command, 26–27
Selection commands, 132
selection process, 122
semicolons, 160
Sheet Options area, 41
Sheets collection, 168
Shortcut Key field, 5, 61
shortcut keys, 60–65
spin button, 180–181
Static command, 179–180
static dates, 11
Step command, 160, 162
storage
  assigning macros to toolbar, 66–71
  assigning shortcut keys to macros, 60–65
  in current workbook, 56–57
  making macros available, 58–59
  in Personal Macro Workbook, 55

protecting macros, 59–60
  VBA modules, 57
  in workbooks, 55–56
Store Macro In field, 5
string operator, 140
Sub lines, 24, 44–45
subroutines
  calling, 93–94
  naming, 92–93
  running macros as, 95–97
  writing, 94–95
Syntax Error message, 135

T

text centering, 32
text manipulation commands, 81–83
text operators, 138
Title argument, 104–105
TODAY formula, 10–12
toggle buttons, 178–180
Toggle Folders button, 21
toolbars
  Developer Ribbon, 2–4, 20
  Quick Access, 66–71
  View, 2
  Visual Basic, 30*f*

Toolbox, 113
Trust Center window, 58

U

Until command, 165
UsedRange method, 168
UserForms
  adding to List Box, 114–116
  offering lists of options, 112–114
  responding to user selection, 116–117

V

value property, 180
values, displaying formulas as
  overview, 36–40
  testing macros, 38
  viewing macro code, 38–40
variables
  arrays
    numbers
      versus names, 143–145
      overview, 142–143
      rules, 145–146
  combining into expressions, 137–138
  creating, 136–137
  naming, 135

variables (*cont.*)
  operators
    arithmetic
      operators, 139
    comparison
      operators, 139
    logical
      operators, 140
    precedence of,
      141–142
    string
      operator, 140
  overview, 106–107,
    134–137
variants, 136
VB Editor. *See* Visual
  Basic Editor
VBA commands, 131–132
vertical lables, 76–78
View Code button, 21, 115
View Macros command, 68
View menu, 88
View Object button, 21, 115
View toolbar, 2
viewing macro code, 38–40
Visual Basic
  customized functions
    hiding sensitive
      data, 101–102
    simplifying
      complicated
      calculations,
      97–101
  displaying formulas
    as values
      overview, 36–38
      testing
        macros, 38

viewing macro
  code, 38–40
harvesting macro
  code
  arrange module
    windows, 45
  constructing
    macros, 45–50
  opening new
    modules, 45
  overview,
    44–51
  removing old
    macros, 50–51
  testing
    macros, 50
macro commands, 80
recording macros,
  40–43
subroutines
  calling, 93–94
  naming, 92–93
  running macros
    as, 95–97
  writing, 94–95
Visual Basic (VB) Editor
  Code window,
    22–23
  modules, 21, 57
  overview, 88–89
  Project Explorer,
    20–21
  Properties window,
    21–22, 174–176,
    181
  Toolbox, 113
  windows in,
    74–75

W

While command, 165
While...Wend
  structure, 166
With Selection command,
  78, 123–124
With structures, 78
With...End With
  command, 47–49
workbooks
  closing, 43–44
  saving, 55–56
  saving to new,
    16–17
worksheets
  adding buttons to,
    172–174
  adding toggle buttons
    to, 178–180
  adjusting control
    properties, 174–176
  changing appearance
    of
      color scheme,
        128–129
      column
        headings,
        122–124
      number
        appearance,
        125–126
      overview,
        126–128
  monthly report,
    12–13
  overview, 171–172
  spin button, 180–181

writing
  code
    for buttons
      and controls,
      176–178
    for input boxes,
      106–108
    for macros, 78
  commands
    overview, 74–80
    paring code,
      78–80

understanding
  code, 78
  subroutines, 94–95

X

XLSM file extensions, 56

Z

zoom buttons
  adding to worksheets,
    172–174

toggle button
  controls, 178–180
  writing code for,
    176–178
ZoomIt_Click event
  handler, 176